# The Gentlemen of Gloucester

## A New Look at the First Troop Philadelphia City Cavalry

# The Gentlemen of Gloucester

## A New Look at the First Troop Philadelphia City Cavalry

by
G. Andrew Meschter (Author)

and
Kenneth Baumel (Executive Editor)

Somewhere it is written, "Honor your father and mother, so you may live long in the land." I therefore dedicate this book to George William and Susan Dell Meschter, my parents.

# Table of Contents

# Acknowledgements

Over the last five years, I burdened many friends and acquaintances for editing help while putting this book together. They read and re-read countless drafts and sections of drafts, offering encouragement and criticism along the way. I therefore offer my sincerest thanks to Charlie Meredith, Peter Clauss, Tyler Hathaway, Rudolph Rauch, Julia Wirts, Tom "Doc" White, James Blunt, John Warlow, Larry Grim, Dennis Boylan, Peter Cachion, David Thayer, Lawrence Field, Lewis Neilsen, Daniel Mannix, Harry Gobora, Edward Greene, Eric and Rebecca Guenther, Alix Cummin, Joseph Seymour, Jason Mayland, John Bansemer, Edward Gallen, Jack Tomarchio, Boysie Turner, Joshua West, Andrew White, Nicholas Gaspari, Max von Mettenheim, Otto von Guben, Fritz von Preussen, Klaus von Dohren, Brandon Adams, Austin Lamac, Kevin Gelzhiser, Ryan Noyes, George Anderson, Joe Moon, Martin Lenk, Karen Garven, Steven Wirts, and Cristina Liebolt.

In addition, with deepest gratitude, I thank everyone who shared their memories and anecdotes with me, including William Rawle, Klaus Naude, John Walton, Clayton Ames, Anwar Kemal, Thomas Farley, Andrew Markle, Larry Swesey, Ralph Ovale, Karl Schoettle, Mitch Harding, Hugh Redditt, Kevin Harper, John Devereux, Andrew Sullivan, Norris Claytor, Stockton Illoway, Evan Hunt, Llewellyn Hunt, Jake Field, Thomas Nace, Nick Bowden, Ted Christiansen, Bruce Maxfield, Jamie Emlen, David Stokes, Charles McIlvaine, Roy West, Edward Ware, Edward Kellogg, Jeanie Walkup, Charles Ingersoll, Rich Diffenderfer, Tony Biddle, Barbie Gallen, Bucky Buchannan, Charlie Davis, George Coates, James Hanlon, John Duffy, Ben Wille, Stephan Burgi, Peter de Reimer, Daniel Ott, Jim Tornetta, Brooke Gottshall, Ron Fenstermacher, Ted Dougherty, Winfield Dougherty, Amanda Meschter, and Kate Lamac. Finally, I thank Jared Castraldi for this book's cover photo.

# Preface

This book is a history of the First Troop Philadelphia City Cavalry, the oldest mounted unit in the United States military. The narrative covers the Troop's story from its founding in 1774 to the Iraq deployment in 2006, with beginning and ending chapters describing my own personal experience. The anecdotes that comprise much of this book were taken first hand from Troop members who spoke from memory. Although this book is non-fiction, it is written for the general public, not scholars. Formal footnotes, references, and bibliography have thus been deliberately omitted. I have listed secondary sources at the end of the narrative as "further reading."

# Chapter 1

# A Military Calling

Why do some boys yearn to be soldiers when they grow up? Samuel Johnson may have answered that question best when he said, *"Every man thinks meanly of himself for not having been a soldier or not having been at sea."*

My love for martial things began early. In fact, I can pinpoint the moment—at age five—when a war movie captured my imagination on Saturday afternoon television. The film may have been *Sands of Iwo Jima,* starring John Wayne, but I can't recall exactly. Entranced after watching it, I wandered outside to find my mother (a tomboy), who was chopping firewood. I said, "Mom, I want to join the Salvation Army!" Correcting me, she replied, "I think you mean the *United States Army.*"

From that day on, military topics had a mystique and allure for me that trumped almost everything else. This curiosity was fueled not only by books and films and playing war games in the woods with neighborhood friends, but also by annual trips to I. Goldberg—a labyrinthine Army-Navy store in Philadelphia—where jumbled heaps of musty-smelling military surplus gear excited the senses and imagination.

As the years passed however, I learned that war is a terrible thing, not something to be glorified. By the time I reached college, I adopted the anti-military attitude common to many American undergraduates, and absorbed the classicist

1

notion that people join the military only if they have no other opportunities in life.

At age 24, while attending graduate school at the University of Durham, in England, I watched the September 11th World Trade Center attacks on television. That event in 2001 rekindled an interest in military service among young people around me. It was thus in Durham that my childhood interest in soldiering was reinvigorated.

A word of description is in order about Durham. As home to the third oldest university in England after Oxford and Cambridge, it is not well known in the United States. With its Norman cathedral and medieval castle facing each other high on a hill, wrapped around by a river forming a horseshoe, its Georgian houses with large windows, narrow alleyways, and winding cobblestone streets, Durham is an almost painfully beautiful place. Because of its physical beauty and traditional collegiate structure, Durham was often a popular fallback (what we Americans call a "safety school") for students who missed getting into Oxford or Cambridge. Like safety schools anywhere, Durham had a somewhat laid-back lifestyle that emphasized work-life balance over scholastic striving. Graduation speeches celebrated the benefits of keeping academics from overshadowing sports and social life. In this regard, Durham reminded me of Philadelphia—an insular place lacking the dynamism and competitive scramble of neighboring New York City and Washington, D.C., but all the more charming for it. Like Philadelphia, Durham's approach to balanced living made it calm, complacent, phlegmatic, and aloof from the driving obsession to get ahead.

*Durham, England. (Photo by Julia Wirts)*

However, as much as I loved Durham, I felt on a gut level that I somehow hadn't earned the right to enjoy such safe and beautiful surroundings.

This feeling became more acute while I was working on my history dissertation. My tutor sent me to Eton College, to research how World War I altered the 19th century concept of the English gentleman. While leafing through old editions of the *Eton College Chronicle* there, I read numerous stories about young Etonians who rushed into military service at the war's outbreak, fought self-sacrificially, and died as a consequence.

Their example has haunted me ever since.

Returning to Durham with a heavy conscience, I felt the urge to become a soldier, to expose myself to the rigors of

3

military training, and to put myself in the pathway of deployment into combat. Perhaps by training for war, I would feel better qualified to enjoy the blessings of peace at such academic havens as Durham.

Just as I was entertaining these thoughts, several people crossed my path in rapid succession who helped further shift my trajectory toward military service.

While embarking on one of those trips to Eton, I saw Peter Balfour on the Durham train platform. Dressed in a smartly cut suit, with umbrella in hand like a swagger stick, he was heading south to meet with members of the cavalry unit he had just joined. He explained that he was following a family tradition for men to serve in the Army for a few years after college, before embarking on their civilian careers.

Balfour and some of his friends taught me that in Britain, military service was a highly respected calling because of its ancient ties with aristocracy. Through this feudal heritage, it was considered normal for gentlemen to want serve in the armed forces. What's more, these men sought combat roles over safe administrative posts.

Inspired by their example, I wanted to do my own bit by serving in the United States military. When I wondered aloud which branch to join, one of Balfour's friends said, "Don't waste your time with the American Army! They have no culture, no flair, and no sense of tradition. You can see that in their dress uniforms. They also emphasize fancy gadgetry over man-to-man leadership." He continued, "The U.S. Marine Corps however are a much different proposition." They understand the human factors in war. They have better discipline, better esprit de corps, they work within tighter financial budgets, and they have *much* better uniforms!" Although I initially laughed off this assessment, on a gut level, I wondered if he was right.

By summer's end, I was tilting towards joining the Marine Corps as an intelligence officer. That role seemed to incorporate the best balance of brains and brawn.

At that juncture, another friend appeared who made me reconsider. His name was Martin. He was a German graduate student in Durham who originally came from Hamburg. Like many Hamburgers, Martin was an extreme Anglophile. And like some of my British friends, he believed that it was a gentleman's duty to be a soldier.

Years earlier, Martin had served in the Bundeswehr (the German Army) before entering Heidelberg University as an undergraduate. Like Peter Balfour, Martin served in a cavalry unit in Luneburg that was a German version of Balfour's fancy Guards regiment in England. Day after day, Martin regaled me with army stories. He described various things he learned to do as a soldier—practical, gritty, down-to-earth things that counterbalanced his ethereal temperament as a scholar—such as commanding armored reconnaissance vehicles, shooting all sorts of weapons, and navigating military bureaucracy with gifts and smooth talk.

Although Martin clearly understood why I wanted to join the Marines, he advised me to abstain from doing so immediately.

In his attempted British accent, he suggested this alternative plan: "Before you run off and join the Marines, why not visit Heidelberg, where I studied at university? I'll put you in touch with people I know there, and you'll gain cultural perspective that can't be got anywhere else. After you soak that up for a while, you can fly back to the States and get brainwashed at boot camp."

With Martin's guidance, I booked the cheapest flight possible on Ryan Air to Frankfurt Hahn (a minor airport, miles from the city of Frankfurt) clutching a rucksack stuffed with items to meet the range of contingents—from outdoor bivouacs to coat-and-tie dinners—which I imagined could occur in continental Europe. Within minutes of landing in Germany, I managed to hitch a ride with a young American couple who proudly owned a newish BMW. Filled with the mortal dread of hitch-hikers common to most Americans, they nervously agreed to give me a lift, took me as far as the first truck stop in sight, and then dispatched me with obvious relief. With no rides from truck drivers forthcoming, I spent that first night sleeping under a bridge in the pouring rain without the faintest idea where I was.

After getting my bearings, I made it to Heidelberg. The city was gorgeous—easily Durham's equal for physical beauty. There I soon met people through Martin's social introductions. Among these was a clean-limbed German girl called Yvonne (not her real name) who studied French and English, stood exactly as tall as I, and was easily the more intelligent of us two. Having been strictly brought up, she adopted me not only as her boyfriend, but as her personal finishing-school project. She accomplished more in two years than my grandmother did in twenty, and she drilled more manners into me than I knew what to do with.

In addition to Yvonne, I also met a number of guys who were part of a Heidelberg student corps called the "Saxon-Prussians." According to them, the last American to drift into their midst had been Mark Twain, who described the experience in his 1880 book *A Tramp Abroad.*

The Saxon-Prussians were quite a find! Many of them had fascinating family histories, some with Prussian grandee forefathers who once had estates in eastern Germany. These they had to abandon when the Soviets overran that area at the end World War II. Having lost everything, their descendants became displaced nobles, whose reduced circumstances led them to cultivate a mixture of courtliness and diffidence. Like Martin in Durham, many of these Saxon-Prussians saw military service as a gentlemanly duty, and they all tended to serve in Martin's Luneburg cavalry unit.

Yvonne knew *all* about the Saxon-Prussians, because her previous boyfriend had been a member, and she understood very well how tempted I was when they asked me to join. This invitation threw a monkey wrench into my plan to join the Marine Corps. For months, she patiently listened to me think aloud as I weighed out the pros and cons of each.

The Saxon-Prussians' main draw was their *camaraderie*—their dedication to getting along with each other in a spirit of candor and selflessness. I hesitated to join them however, because my deeper desire was to become a soldier. The drumbeat of that older childhood call refused to be silenced.

Then one night, Yvonne wisely said, "Drew, I know how much it would mean for you to join the Saxon Prussians, but you are American and they are German. It doesn't make sense for you to join them unless you plan to stay here for life. They are not just a fraternity; they are part of an extended family. They intentionally tend to marry each other's sisters and cousins! You should try to find an *American* version of the Saxon-Prussians. Is there anything in the U.S. that combines what you like about the Saxon-Prussians with your desire to be a soldier?"

She was dead right, and her question caught me off guard. Could there possibly be an American version of what I had just witnessed in England and Germany?

Choosing to not join the Saxon-Prussians was hard to do, and I postponed making that decision until the last possible minute. That moment occurred on the first night of the upcoming university semester, at a ceremony welcoming their newest members. On that fascinating evening, as old boys of all ages made toasts and sang traditional songs by candlelight in a room dramatically decorated with framed silhouettes of past members, I felt for a few hours as if I were one of them. At the end of the night however, I mustered the courage to say, "Unless I can join you with full commitment for life, I don't want to join you at all. I must remain your guest and not become a member."

Leaving the house feeling very alone, I rode home that night singing one of their songs—*So Punktlich zur Sekunde*— with tears streaming down my face as my bicycle tires bounced along the quiet cobblestone streets. That song would linger in mind for years afterward, stirring and manly in the way they sang it while standing on tables and chairs, with the end of each line clipped off in the Teutonic fashion. Having closed one surprising chapter in life, I now wondered what could possibly come next.

Then something bubbled up from my memory. Years before, I stumbled upon a magazine article about an eccentric

Philadelphia-based National Guard unit unlike any other in the United States. Founded in colonial times—when Pennsylvania still belonged to the Hanoverian King George—it was as much a gentleman's social club as it was an army combat unit. According to that article, its members rode horses, wore fancy uniforms, and served as cavalry scouts. Come to think of it, they seemed like an American version of Peter's and Martin's cavalry units in Britain and Germany. Although the details from that magazine article were vivid, I couldn't recall any names. Did they still exist? After searching and cross-referencing various terms for a while on the Internet, I finally found them. The organization was called the *First Troop Philadelphia City Cavalry*. They were still alive and kicking— and they had been there all along in my native Pennsylvania!

Alive with hope, I sent their adjutant an overly worded email, asking if they were seeking new members. After hitting "Send" however, weeks passed by—and then months—with no response. My hope faded.

Then one day, an email appeared in my inbox from Tom Farley, the Troop's adjutant. He explained that they had just been deployed to Bosnia, where spotty email service prevented him from keeping up with correspondence. He welcomed me to visit the Troop's headquarters in Philadelphia any time I wanted.

While home for Christmas that year, my sister Kate and I ventured into town to see First City Troop Armory. Like Philadelphia itself, the building was easy to overlook at first glance, but surprisingly opulent the more you took in the details.

Upon entering the Armory through the portico, Kate and I noticed two white marble plaques facing each other on opposite walls. The plaques were both engraved in clean black Roman print and listed the names of each First City Troop captain since 1774. We looked at each other a bit wide-eyed, impressed by the sense of continuity between past and present represented on those simple slabs. That sense of continuity went deeper than the names written in stone. We later learned that the tablets had been placed there and were still maintained by the H. C. Wood Company—a fifth-generation family-owned firm with strong ties to the Troop.

*Marble plaques donated to the Armory by the H.C Wood Company. (Author's photo)*

As we stood there, two First City Troop members walked up to greet us. One of them was dressed in a suit like a stockbroker, the other in working clothes like a carpenter. They shook our hands affably and offered to give us a quick tour of the place, explaining that this armory building was the only remaining National Guard installation in the United States built with private funds and still occupied by its founding unit. There had once been fancy armories like this one up and down the East Coast, but this was the last of its type still used for its originally intended purpose.

Beyond the portico, a drill hall stretched nearly a football field in length. Originally used as a riding ring for horses, it was now a parking lot for civilian and military vehicles. (Free parking in town was a perk for unit members.) A large mirror high on one wall, which a century ago had been installed for men to check their posture while on horseback, still served its intended purpose when Troopers brought horses into the ring for their frequent ceremonial rides through town.

*Troopers prepare for a turnout in the Armory's drill hall. Note the riding mirror on the far wall. (Photo by Andrew Colket)*

Our hosts began the tour by taking us upstairs to the third-floor mess hall, a high-ceilinged room with large windows, adorned with various flags and portraits of Troop captains past. When Kate noticed that some of the paintings were fifteen feet tall, while others were only a fraction of that size, one of the men laughingly explained that the smaller portraits reflected Troopers' reduced spending power after the advent of income tax. The other added that by tradition, each Troop captain must commission his own portrait painted at private expense. He may keep it for life, but must then will it to the Armory upon death.

*The mess hall. (Photo by Tevebaugh and Associates)*

Our hosts pointed out the Troop captain's chair—an exact replica of the one used by George Washington at the Constitutional Convention in 1787, which Benjamin Franklin famously described as having a rising sun on it, as opposed to a setting sun. Only three of these chairs exist, including the one at Independence Hall. By tradition, only Troop captains or Presidents of the United States may sit in it. Theodore Roosevelt sat there in 1907.

*Troop Captain's chair, one of three in existence, copied from the "rising sun" chair used by George Washington at the Constitutional Convention in 1787. (Author's photo)*

They took us downstairs to the Troop's Museum—said to be the oldest and most comprehensive collection belonging to any one military unit in the United States. Again, the underlying theme here was *continuity*. Each item in the collection had been privately purchased and used by a member of the unit. Because Troopers over the years could afford to buy the best, many of the weapons, uniforms, and items on display exhibited exceptional workmanship. Among the most impressive artifacts were the Troop's original silk standard (battle flag), made in 1775, a portrait of George Washington, painted during his lifetime, and the Chippendale chair and silver beer mug belonging to Abraham Markoe, the unit's founding captain.

*During our first Armory tour, this haunting portrait seemed to stare back at us, regardless of the angle from which it was viewed. Our hosts explained that its subject, Samuel Goodman, Jr., had once been one of Philadelphia's most eligible bachelors. While demonstrating jujitsu moves to friends in the hayloft above the drill hall in 1905, he slipped, fell to the drill floor, and died later from injuries. (Author's photo)*

Impressed with the Armory tour, I felt certain that this was the American fraternity/ military unit that Yvonne had described so prophetically. I decided to join up—if they would have me...

At this point however, before I continue with an account of my subsequent experiences with the First City Troop, let's back up two hundred and forty years, to learn more about the unit from its very beginning.

# Chapter 2

# The Gentlemen of Gloucester

On November 17th, 1774, twenty eight prominent young Philadelphians met at Carpenters Hall in the wake of the First Continental Congress to organize a new cavalry unit that would serve Congress in its efforts to resist perceived threats from Great Britain.

Calling their new unit the *Light Horse of the City of Philadelphia*, they elected their own members and officers by vote, and agreed to pay for their military expenses with their own private funds.

Many of these gentlemen already knew each other as members of the Gloucester Fox Hunting Club, which gathered once or twice a week across the Delaware River from Philadelphia in Gloucester, New Jersey to chase foxes throughout the local countryside. On occasion, they roamed as far east as the Jersey shore. Physically fit and well-conditioned to the saddle, their familiarity with regional terrain made them excellent raw material for becoming cavalry scouts.

Because the Gloucester Hunt formed such a strong foundation for the Philadelphia Light Horse, I think of them both as "the Gentlemen of Gloucester." So complete was the shared identity between both organizations that its members chose Gloucester's official club colors—brown, buff, and gold—as the regimental colors for their new cavalry troop, and they adapted their normal fox-hunting dress for cavalry use.

*Founding members of the Philadelphia Light Horse assemble for drill wearing the modified Gloucester Fox Hunting Club uniform consisting of short brown coat, lined and faced in white and black hat, decorated with a silver cord and jaunty buck's tail. Each man carries privately purchased armaments, including a carbine and cavalry sword slung from the shoulders on white leather cross belts, and a brace of pistols kept in saddle holsters. (Troop Centennial History, 1874)*

17

Light horse cavalrymen were a unique type of soldier in the 18th century. Although trained to fight whenever they engaged with enemy forces of equal or weaker strength, their main job was to provide communication, skirmishing, and reconnaissance support to higher levels of command. Performing most of these operations deep inside enemy territory, they had to be improvisational and quick thinking. Members of the Philadelphia Light Horse approached this military role with an entrepreneurial spirit borne of their civilian experiences. As commercial and professional men, they were accustomed to conducting complicated and risky business ventures on a handshake basis with contacts throughout the British Empire.

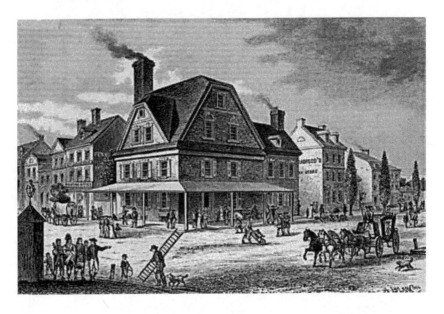

*The London Coffee House, Philadelphia's most popular colonial business hub, where the Gloucester Fox Hunting Club was formed in 1766, and where members of the Philadelphia Light Horse met to conduct military and civilian affairs. (The Library Company of Philadelphia)*

*No images survive of the original Gloucester huntsmen in action, but some Troopers still hunt today. Bennett Opitz (above), who discovered the Troop through his love of foxhunting, said, "Fox hunting made me want to become a modern Cavalry Scout in the U.S. Army. It taught me to navigate unfamiliar terrain while taking calculated risks, in pursuit of an adversary—in this case, a fox." (Photo from Bennett Opitz)*

Abraham Markoe was the Troop's founding organizer and first elected captain. Hailing from enterprising French Huguenot stock, he was a merchant and landowner, whose family grew cane sugar in the West Indies. Although he had no military experience prior to the formation of the Philadelphia Light Horse, his peers elected him captain because of his intelligence, enthusiasm, and business leadership skills.

He commissioned the Troop's first regimental standard—a yellow silk flag featuring a British Union Jack in the upper left corner. Soon after receiving this flag, the men agreed to alter it by covering the Union Jack with thirteen horizontal stripes representing each of the Anglo-American colonies. According to Philadelphia tradition, this was the first recorded use of the thirteen stripe motif that has been a defining feature in American flags ever since. This layering of British flag and American stripes seems almost prophetic in retrospect, reminding us today that Troop is still a cultural melding of the New World and Mother England.

*The Philadelphia Light Horse regimental standard. Full color digital image available on www.gentlemenofgloucester.com. (Troop Centennial History, 1874)*

The standard also featured a unit crest in the center, with a horse's head representing *cavalry* and thirteen ribbons tied in a knot representing the *unity* of the American colonies. A colonist, disguised as a Native American, symbolically represented *liberty*, while his unstrung bow indicated a *readiness for war* and *preference for peace*. His Phrygian cap also represented liberty. An angel blowing a trumpet symbolized *fame*. A decorative ribbon beneath spelled out the Troop's motto, "For These We Strive."

*Among America's oldest surviving flags, the original 1775 Troop standard is enshrined in the Armory's museum today. Close inspection reveals that the thirteen stripes in the upper left corner cover a British Union Jack. In a certain sense, the Troop is still a cultural melding of North America and Mother England. (Author's photo)*

In the spring of 1776, when hostilities broke out between Great Britain and the American colonies, Markoe discovered that a neutrality pact between Denmark and Britain exposed his family to the confiscation of their property in St. Croix (a part of the Danish West Indies at the time), if he took an active role in the up-coming war for independence. To preserve his family's holdings, he resigned from the Light Horse, and became the first man named to the Troop's Honorary Roll.

In Markoe's place, the men elected Samuel "Christian Sam" Morris as their new captain. An exuberant personality, and Master of the Gloucester Hunt, Morris was described by contemporaries as a man "devoted to manly exercises and the sports of the field." Although raised as a pacifist member of the Society of Friends (Quakers), Morris believed enough in the cause of American independence to fight for it. The Quakers read him out of meeting when he joined the Troop, but Morris retained Quaker dress, manners, and worship habits for the rest of his life.

# Chapter 3

# The American Revolution

In 1775, Continental Congress assigned the Philadelphia Light Horse with its first mission: to escort newly appointed general—George Washington—on his ride north from Philadelphia to assume command of the Continental Army outside Boston. The Troop accompanied Washington as far as New York City, building a friendly acquaintance with him along the way that would last long after the war. When Martha Washington later passed through Philadelphia to visit her husband on campaign, the Troop escorted her as well.

Trusting the Troopers' business acumen and financial experience, Congress often sent them to carry cash payments to Continental armies afield. A Light Horse detachment delivering money to Benedict Arnold in Quebec sustained the unit's first two casualties when one of its members fell in combat and another fatally shot himself with his own pistol—while it was still in its holster. Modern wags cite this anecdote as proof that the First City Troop's bi-polar tendencies toward valiance on one hand and buffoonery on the other have been part of the unit's culture since the very beginning.

Soon after taking command of the Continental Army, Washington suffered a string of defeats. Through a series of narrow escapes in New York, he withdrew from Manhattan, and wended his way south through New Jersey with the British in pursuit. In battles and skirmishes during this difficult period, many Continental soldiers were captured and held in British prison ships where they faced thirst, starvation, and disease. Colonial fighters who escaped capture endured other hardships. Half clothed, often barefoot, low on ammunition, and lacking adequate provisions, hospitals, and shelter, many suffered death and disease from exposure.

*In addition to their military service, members of the Philadelphia Light Horse contributed to American independence in a number of indirect but surprising ways. Thomas Jefferson wrote the Declaration of Independence on a lap desk (above) built by cabinetmaker (and Trooper) Benjamin Randolph. And Trooper Jonathan Dunlap printed the first broadsides of that document for official distribution on the night of July 4, 1776. (Author's photo of Jefferson's lap desk at the Museum of American History in Washington DC)*

By the autumn of 1776, the American cause was in crisis and facing collapse. Retreating into Pennsylvania, Washington put the Delaware River between his army and the British, and wondered what to do next. To escape the threatening British advance on Philadelphia, Continental

Congress abandoned its headquarters there and set up a provisional capital in Baltimore.

United States Army historian and First City Troop member Joseph Seymour explains that as Washington's army retreated south from New York toward Philadelphia, the Light Horse "urged their horses north through roads clogged with colonial deserters and refugees heading in the other direction." The Light Horse arrived at Trenton on December 2nd, 1776 just as Washington's prospects seemed most dire, and immediately began probing the British lines in New Jersey for him.

In a desperate gamble to prevent the collapse of his army, Washington decided to make a counter strike into New Jersey. With many of his soldiers' enlistments about to expire at year's end, he had to move quickly. On December 23rd, he ordered a daring three-pronged attack on the Hessian garrison at Trenton, commanded by Colonel Johann Gottlieb Rall.

On Christmas evening, Washington's forces began crossing the Delaware River at sunset. Because of the river's tides, drifting sheets of ice, driving sleet, and strong winds, half the American force failed to make it across that night—but the Philadelphia Light Horse succeeded. They crossed part of the river by boat, and when compacted ice blocked their path on the far side, they took to the water on horseback, fording the rest of the way with floating ice brushing their saddle leather.

*Washington crosses the Delaware River to attack Trenton. The Troop accompanied him on this mission. (The Library Company of Philadelphia)*

Once ashore, Washington's men—some of them barefoot—trudged nine miles inland to attack a Hessian mercenary force in Trenton on the morning of December 26th. Riding with Major General Nathaniel Greene, the Philadelphia Light Horse helped Washington's men surround the Hessian compound and capture its defenders.

During that battle, Cornet John Dunlap and a detachment of Troopers attacked a group of Hessians defending a fortified barn. Surrounding the barn from a distance, he and his men called for their surrender, and some parley, the Hessians complied. While taking some Hessian officers into custody, Dunlap secured gorges and breastplates as war trophies from them that remain in the First City Troop's museum collection today.

Surprised at his own success, Washington withdrew back to Pennsylvania to prepare for a second offensive into

New Jersey. On December 29th, he crossed the Delaware again to attack the British at Princeton. To gather intelligence for this advance, he dispatched a Philadelphia Light Horse patrol led by Colonel Joseph Reed to hunt for British prisoners to bring back for questioning.

Moving cautiously to avoid their own capture, the Troopers stole into enemy territory and, to their surprise, soon discovered a British foraging party from the 16th (Queen's) Light Dragoons. After trailing the dragoons' wagons and men for a distance, Reed and his Troopers suddenly rushed them when the enemy started plundering a stone farmhouse. After a short standoff, the dragoons surrendered. The Troopers forced their prisoners at gunpoint to mount their horses behind them, and then galloped back to American lines as other British dragoons rode after them in pursuit. Burdened with extra riders and captured weapons, they reached the American pickets with only one mishap—Trooper James Caldwell's mount threw him.

From these prisoners, Washington learned that General Cornwallis planned to trap him on the banks of the Delaware River. Washington countered Cornwallis by ordering a flanking movement to attack the British rear guard at Princeton on January 3rd. Following an all-night forced march, the Americans reached Princeton just before dawn and attacked, capturing 194 prisoners after a short fight at Nassau Hall.

Elated with his victories and the capture of much-needed supplies, Washington lacked cavalry strength to pursue the British for a full rout. But he deployed the cavalry he had on hand—which happened to be the Philadelphia Light Horse. While riding down the retreating enemy, Washington joined the Gentlemen of Gloucester and cut loose, shouting, "It is a fine fox chase, my boys!"

As Washington withdrew his forces from Princeton, he tasked Captain Morris and the Philadelphia Light Horse to remain behind with an artillery detachment to guard the American rear. As the American artillerymen, lacking horses, slowly made way pulling their cannon by hand with forty men to a gun, a Queen's Light Dragoons detachment rode in to attack. Morris dismounted with his Troopers to form a line across the road to defend them. The Redcoats rode up to within view of the Troopers, paused for a beat to size up their resolve, and then withdrew without firing a shot.

On their way home from Princeton a Light Horse detachment stopped by John Morton's house near Moorestown for a visit. After exchanging pleasantries, Morton told the Troopers that he would hide two quarter casks of Madeira at the bottom of his cellar steps later that night—one for themselves and one for General Washington. Returning under the cover of darkness to secure the wine, the Troopers were intercepted by a British cavalry patrol just as they were lifting the casks from the cellar. Refusing to allow good Madeira to fall into enemy hands (and displaying a sense of priorities common to Troopers ever since), they held the British at bay and managed to escape with both barrels intact.

(It's worth mentioning that even today Madeira has resonance among Philadelphians who care about the city's colonial heritage. Although the wine has not been widely popular in the United States since Prohibition, some make a point of drinking it as a nod to colonial forebears—real or imagined. When the Wall Street Journal wrote an article describing a resurgence of Madeira's popularity in 2015, such

Philadelphia patriots welcomed the news, but hoped it wouldn't cause prices to spike.)

Happy with the Troop's performance during his successful campaign (and grateful, no doubt, for the Madeira), Washington penned the following letter to Captain Morris, an eighteenth-century copy of which (printed on silk cloth) remains in the Troop museum today:

> *"I take this Opportunity of returning my most sincere thanks to the Captain and to the Gentlemen who compose the Troop, for the many essential services which they have rendered to their Country, and to me personally, during the Course of this severe Campaign. Though composed of Gentlemen of Fortune, they have shewn a noble Example of Discipline and Subordination, and in several actions have shewn a Spirit of Bravery which will even do Honor to them and will ever greatly be remembered by me. "*

There wasn't much time for celebrating. General Sir William Howe marched on Philadelphia in September of 1777, and the Troop served General Washington and the Marquis de Lafayette during the battles of Brandywine and Germantown. Although Germantown ended in American defeat, their resolve helped convince the French to enter the war against Britain.

*Annual Battle of Germantown reenactment at Cliveden, the Chew family's ancestral home. In 1777, a Philadelphia Light Horse detachment arrested Benjamin Chew as British Loyalist. Letting bygones be bygones, later generations of Chews joined the First City Troop. (Photo by Stephen Ujifusa)*

Throughout the Philadelphia campaign, Washington employed the Philadelphia Light Horse as his bodyguard and intelligence service, giving each Trooper a special pass allowing the bearer to cross American lines at will. According to tradition, they were the only unit Washington afforded such uncircumscribed trust. The Troop Museum retains one of these passes today in its permanent collection.

The British occupied Philadelphia until June of 1778. While American forces wintered at Valley Forge, small Light Horse detachments preformed missions for Lafayette, the Continental Congress, and the Council of Safety, carrying dispatches and cash payments to armies scattered afield.

When facing their British dragoon adversaries throughout the war, the Philadelphia Light Horse—amateurs all—must have acutely felt their limitations as non-professional soldiers. Indeed, fox hunting and part-time drill were their only military training. But that preparation proved adequate. They never confronted a British cavalry unit without overcoming or equaling them. In his book *Democracy in America*, Alexis de Tocqueville provided a clue that may help explain this success. He observed that in democratic armies where military discipline attempts to guide individual expression and not destroy it, "the obedience that results is less precise but more enthusiastic and intelligent. It is rooted in the will of the person who obeys. It does not rely solely on his instinct but also on his reason, so it will frequently tighten up by itself as the danger calls for it. The discipline of an aristocratic army [as in 18th century Britain] is likely to be relaxed in war, because this discipline is based on habits, which war disrupts."

In addition to their military services, Troopers aided the American cause by helping to finance it. When the Bank of North America raised £300,000 for the Continental Army, twenty seven Troopers pledged sums ranging from £1000 to £10,000 per man (approximately $250,000 to $2,500,000 in today's money). On multiple occasions, the First City Troop's founding generation set an example of donating large sums of money in an almost flagrant manner. This cavalier ethos of "financial bravery" would eventually become a hallmark of the unit's culture for generations to come.

# Chapter 4

# The Federal Period

When the dust settled after the Revolutionary War, Philadelphia found itself standing tall (albeit, not for very long) as North America's primate city—the combined commercial, cultural, and political capital.

*First City Troopers ride on Philadelphia's Market Street in 1799. (The Library Company of Philadelphia)*

As the city's premier military unit, the Philadelphia Light Horse—now renamed the *First Troop Philadelphia City Cavalry*—served as a combined defense force, constabulary, and honor guard, attracting luminaries into its ranks with easy magnetism.

According to the *American Daily Advertiser,* the first successful daily newspaper in the United States (founded by a Trooper), "the lowest ranking privates in the Troop were principal officers of the state government, officers who had commanded regiments in the Continental Army, merchants of the most respectable characters, lawyers of eminent talents and property." Among these notables were Philadelphia mayors Samuel Miles and Robert Wharton; John Dunlap and D. C. Claypoole, whose Congressional publishing firm Dunlap & Claypoole first printed the Declaration of Independence, Constitution, and Washington's farewell address; John Maxwell Nesbitt, a founder of the Insurance Company of North America; William Ward Burrows, the first Commandant of the United States Marine Corps; Jonathan Williams, the first Superintendent of the United States Military Academy at West Point; and William Rush, who as Secretary of State, established the United States/Canadian border through the Rush-Bagot Convention of 1818.

Although the Troop would later come to be associated with Philadelphia's old-money patriciate, its eighteenth-century members were equal parts brash and genteel, much like the Founding Fathers in general. Seeking to preserve the stylistic trappings of the English class system, they also wanted open access for talented newcomers. Ethnically, they tended to be of Scots-Irish, English, and Welsh descent— Presbyterians, Anglicans, and undogmatic Quakers who were well-to-do, but not upper crust.

Their budding influence sparked envy among those who were both more and less privileged. While Quaker grandees, whose pacifist ideals excluded them from power during the Revolution, resented Troopers who assumed social prominence in the city after the war, republican factions saw their professional, social, and political influence as a threat to democracy. Navigating these shoals, Troopers cultivated understated, Quaker-like manners and gave generously to philanthropies. For example, when Congress gave back pay to soldiers who had served in the Continental Army from 1776 through 1783, the First City Troop voted to pool their share in the money to establish the Foundling Hospital for children orphaned by the war.

*As the first Commandant of the United States Marine Corps, William Ward Burrows founded the Marine Corps band, and established a cultural emphasis on thrift and physical fitness that have characterized that branch of service ever since. (Photo of print donated to the Armory by Roy West)*

In 1794, the Troop jumped at the chance to deploy with their beloved George Washington when, as President of the

United States, he mobilized 13,000 militiamen from four states to subdue the Whiskey Rebellion in western Pennsylvania. Almost two centuries later, when that short and successful mission was portrayed in the 1984 TV miniseries *George Washington,* a number of First City Troopers were cast as extras in the film. According to Edward Gallen, studio people on set where astonished to discover that he and his friends were not historical re-enactors as had been supposed, but direct descendants of men who served with Washington on that campaign.

In 1814, during the War of 1812, the Troop was deployed to monitor British warship movements on the Chesapeake Bay.

Accompanying the unit was Robert Wharton, a former Troop captain who had since become Brigadier General of the Pennsylvania Militia and mayor of Philadelphia. Having held these lofty positions, Wharton entered Troop folklore by re-enlisting back into the Troop at the rank of *private.* In doing so, he followed the eccentric custom of "rank flip-flopping," a term I use that has characterized the First City Troop since its founding.

Wharton's decision to deploy, which received general applause at first, assumed legendary proportions when one morning, while taking his turn as the unit's cook, a courier rode up to inform him that he had just been re-elected as mayor of Philadelphia—*in absentia*. Bitterly disappointed that he had to leave his Troop comrades, he delivered what one account described as "a pathetic [sad] farewell address" before reluctantly returning home to assume his mayoral duties. Wharton was ultimately elected five times to the office of mayor—more than any other person in Philadelphia history.

The War of 1812 occurred at a time when Philadelphia began declining in relative importance to other American cities. The United States capital shifted to Washington D.C., New York City surged ahead as the nation's financial center, and Philadelphia settled into provincial middle age, taking the First City Troop along with it.

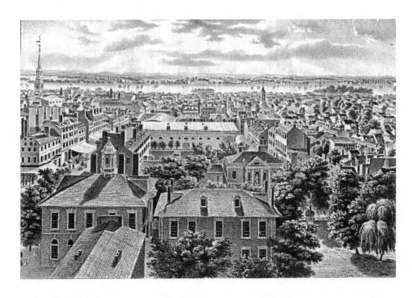

*By the 1830s, "mild" Philadelphia was no longer America's primate city, having lost financial preeminence to New York City, and political headship to Washington D.C. (The Library Company of Philadelphia)*

But as the old saying goes, "poverty preserves." That is, cities often mellow and grow charming once they lose their preeminence. When a once-bustling metropolis becomes an insular backwater, its citizens tend to relish older ways of doing things, just as they preserve the old buildings and architecture that remind them of former glory years. According to Philadelphia historian (and First City Trooper) Nicholas Wainwright, when Philadelphia lost its prominence as

America's primate city, it grew complacent, relaxed, and comfortable, with "easy-going Southern overtones... in marked contrast to the hurly-burly, and the raucous bustle of [her successor] New York."

As commercial supremacy passed to New York, Philadelphia's shipping merchants drew closer to their counterparts in the South. When well-to-do Virginians and South Carolinians visited Philadelphia for annual shopping and cultural trips, Philadelphians were easily charmed by their dress and manners, which originally stemmed from cavalier England. Families from these two regions frequently intermarried, and their sons joined the First City Troop. This infusion from regions rich in military tradition (home to Virginia Military Institute and The Citadel) helps explain why a combat unit like the Troop became such an established fixture in Quaker-formed Philadelphia.

With overlapping social connections and business partnerships, along with the camaraderie built through military drill each week, Troopers passed their affinity for the unit to their children, cousins, and friends. Within two generations of its founding, the Troop was not just a military unit anymore, but an extended family.

In 1824, the Marquis de Lafayette returned to America to see the new republic and visit old friends from the Revolution. While in Philadelphia, he designed a dramatic new uniform for the First City Troop featuring a Prussian blue tunic, white breeches, black boots, and a bearskin crested helmet that remains in use as the Troop's full dress uniform today. That uniform, perhaps more than any other symbol, has helped to visually unite each Troop generation into one cultural and historic identity.

*Lafayette's uniform—a generational motif. (First City Troop collection)*

As Philadelphia industrialized, and its population grew with immigration and urban crowding, a string of riots broke out in the city during the 1830s, 40s, and 50s. Violent neighborhood gangs with such colorful names as the Moyamensing Killers and Blood Tubs exacerbated the problem. Their members infiltrated Philadelphia's volunteer fire companies, fighting each other just as readily as they fought fires. Since Philadelphia did not have a police force at that time, the Troop and other militia units were often called to help disperse these riots and mobs.

*Street riots in 1844. (The Library Company of Philadelphia)*

During that period, Philadelphians of all stripes sought refuge from social conflict by forming small private clubs, with memberships falling along ethnic, class, and religious lines. Although by definition each of these organizations was exclusive, it was the rare citizen who couldn't find one to suit his own interests and temperament. In 1834, some Troopers helped form the Philadelphia Club, first gentlemen's town club in the United States. Like the Schuylkill Fishing Company (an angling society formed in 1732 and still active today), the Philadelphia Club would retain an umbilical connection to the Troop for generations to come.

# Chapter 5

# The Civil War

When the Civil War broke out in 1861, the First City Troop was among the first units to respond to President Lincoln's call up for ninety-day militia. At Falling Water, Virginia, they fought in the first cavalry skirmish of the entire war, facing a wily colonel from the Army of Northern Virginia who would later become famous as "Stonewall Jackson." The Union Army would use this engagement as a case study for officer training later in the war.

Military life came as a rude shock to some of the more pampered Troopers, but they adjusted good-humoredly. Bankers, doctors, lawyers, and society dandies alike carried water up slippery streambanks in heavy iron buckets, dug latrine trenches, and tended muddy horses after each day's march. Rigid camp discipline was hard for men who had always been free to do as they pleased, but they made it a point of honor to follow military regulations and submit to the chain of command.

All of this built tremendous comradery. As the Troop's centennial history would observe, "With gentlemen, it was only necessary to notice quietly any little infraction of duty, and no punishments were ever inflicted. Many humorous incidents hardly worthy of a passing notice in print, constantly recall themselves to those who took part in the campaign, when a few old comrades get together to talk over the events of 1861."

*When the Troop mustered for service in 1861, they took to the field wearing regulation United States Army dragon uniforms, instead of their much less practical full dress from Lafayette. (First City Troop collection)*

Upon returning home to Philadelphia after this three-month deployment, a number of Troopers left the Active Roll to form new regiments from scratch. Lieutenant R. Butler founded the Second Pennsylvania Cavalry, while another group helped establish the picturesque Sixth Pennsylvania "Rush's" Lancers—the only cavalry unit North or South to ride into combat bearing lances. By war's end, the Troop boasted two Major Generals and nine Brigadiers. As these men left the Active Roll, new enlistees joined up to fill their places.

In 1863, the Troop built its first armory in Philadelphia at 21st and Ash (now Ludlow) Streets. Prior to that, unit members held their meetings at taverns, townhouses, country houses, the Schuylkill Fishing Company, or outdoors in the saddle. Because the Troop's culture took root for decades before it had a physical home, there remains a sense today that the organization's spirit exists more through networks and relationships than it does through fixed settings.

*The Troop's first armory was built in 1863 at 21st and Ash Street (now Ludlow). (The Library Company of Philadelphia)*

When Confederates forces invaded Pennsylvania in 1863, the Pennsylvania militia mobilized in response. Samuel J. Randall, who had served in the Battle of Falling Water three years earlier as a private and who had since been elected to the United States House of Representatives, now commanded the Troop on its second deployment in the war.

Reaching Gettysburg at 4 a.m. in the midst of a violent rainstorm, Troopers spent subsequent weeks reconnoitering local roads, living in the saddle, averaging four hours of sleep per night. While patrolling the Chambersburg Turnpike, they were the first Union unit to encounter J.E.B. Stuart's cavalry corps. Galloping towards enemy lines, they exchanged shots with Confederates, taking prisoners whenever possible. On one occasion, Troopers were nearly enveloped by a superior Confederate force but narrowly escaped capture—and the probable slow death typical of prisoner of war camps during the Civil War.

These skirmishes delayed the Confederate advance for several days, until the Confederates discovered that they were only dealing with small militia patrols and not skirmishers from the main body of the Army of the Potomac. Word of this enemy contact, relayed to Governor Curtin and thence to Washington D.C., was the first indication the Union Army received that a major Confederate force was near Gettysburg.

As battle-hardened Confederates closed in on the Susquehanna River Bridge at Wrightsville, Troopers rode through Union formations attempting to retain order as the infantry ranks nearly collapsed in panic. To prevent a Confederate advance across the mile-long bridge, four Troopers joined a detail to burn the viaduct, feverously working under enemy fire. This action eliminated the chance of an enemy march on Philadelphia, but it was not without controversy. After the war, questions arose about whether the Troopers acted on orders, or whether they took initiative to burn the tax-payer's bridge on their own.

# Chapter 6

# Centennial

In the wake of the Civil War, the Troop's membership dropped to an all-time low. For a time, it seemed like the unit might disband. But the extended Troop family had deep enough roots in Philadelphia that a new generation of enlistees soon replenished the Active Roll.

By this point the Troop was well-known for its flamboyant characters—both respectable and roguish. Take Alfred du Pont Jessup, Jr. for example, a well-to-do young man who served as a private under Captain Samuel Randall during the Gettysburg campaign. After the Civil War, Jessup set off on a global circumnavigation to see the world, but was forced to abandon his plans when, in Alexandria, Egypt he learned that his mother had taken ill. He returned home to care for her, set himself up for a while as a Philadelphia businessman, and then later went out West to be a stock farmer. According to Troop lore, he would spend his winters living lavishly in Philadelphia, and would go back out west each spring for long safari-like hunting trips to shoot big game. One autumn he didn't return home. Official records say he was killed in a duel at River Bend, Colorado, but old Troop hands know better. They insist that on his supposed "hunting" expeditions, Jessup had actually been robbing banks to finance his high-living back home. He finally met his end when a bank heist went awry.

In 1873, the Troop commissioned an obscure local architect called Frank Furness to design a new addition to its armory building. A Congressional Medal of Honor recipient in Rush's Lancers, where other Troopers had also served, Furness expanded the Armory into a fanciful Victorian extravaganza, half clubhouse and half crusader castle, with angular red-and-black brick walls set on a sturdy basement of rubble-faced blue stone. The building was finished in time for the Troop's 1874 centennial celebrations, and eventually triggered a national craze for medieval armories that lasted well into the twentieth century, leaving crenelated regimental buildings in many large American cities today.

At the building's dedication service, St. Peter's Episcopal Church Rector Thomas F. Davies commended the Troop for preserving "manliness" among affluent citizens whose wealth might otherwise tempt them to sensual indulgence, selfish gratification, and "luxurious ease." According to Davies, "The effect of our modern civilization is neither to nurture manliness nor strength... the increase of luxury and splendor of living and great accumulations of wealth, which, unless carefully watched and guarded against, will go far to sap the foundations of both national and individual strength."

The following day, the Active Roll placed Davies' sermon in their collective "pend file" as they sat down in full dress to eat a massive banquet, the menu for which is shown on the following page, using china dining service specially commissioned for the event and drinking imported champagne, privately labeled *Champagne FTPCC*. (The FTPCC label would remain a Troop standard for decades. By one account, the unit continued to serve FTPCC-labeled champagne at formal occasions well into the 1960s.)

1774                                    1874

# CENTENNIAL BANQUET.

## FIRST TROOP
## PHILADELPHIA CITY CAVALRY.

*NOVEMBER 17th, 1874.*

## BILL OF FARE.

Oysters on Shell.

LATOUR BLANCHE.                    CHATEAU Y'QUEM.

Julienne Soup.        Soup à la Reine.

SHERRY.

Boiled Salmon, Lobster Sauce.        Baked Rock, Madeira Sauce.

LIEBFRAUMILCH.        HOCHEIMER.

Filet de Bœuf.        Hot Boned Turkey.

Vegetables.

CHAMPAGNE, " F. T. P. C. C."

Paté à la Financière.

Sweet Breads and Peas.        Croquettes.

Roman Punch frozen in Oranges.

Boned Pheasants.        Roast Grouse.
Boned Partridges.        Roast Quail.

Terrapin.

CHAMPAGNE FRAPPE, " F. T. P. C. C."

Canvasback Ducks.

MADEIRA.

Lettuce.        Fried Oysters.        Paté de Foies Gras.
Roquefort Cheese.        Crackers.

CHAMBERTIN.

Ices.        Jellies.        Charlotte Russe,        Meringues.
Fruits.        Almonds.        Raisins,        Confections.

Coffee.

LIQUEURS.

Piece Montée.

Cigars.        Cigarettes.

COGNAC.        WHISKEY.

*The Armory's 1873 Frank Furness addition included a fireproof safe, an elevator, a fire pump with a hose long enough to reach any part of the building, a large target on one wall in the riding hall for pistol practice, a rifle range along another wall with an iron target fourteen feet wide by sixteen feet high, and a chandelier in the style of ancient armor, manufactured by Caldwell & Company. For their 1874 centennial, Troopers transformed the riding hall's dirt floor into a garden with live plants, fountains, statuary, and walkways. A "brilliant crowd" of well-dressed ladies, gents, and high-ranking Army and Navy officers strolled these paths, eating heavy hors d'oeuvres and admiring Abraham Markoe's original 1775 silk regimental standard, enshrined behind glass in a fire-proof case. (First City Troop collection)*

*The Troop sourced champagne from various producers over the years and affixed its own label. Honorary Trooper Robert Bodine bottled the example above from his own winery for the unit's 1974 Bicentennial. (Photo from Alix Rockwell Jacobs)*

Five years after the great centennial banquet, a pair of Troopers gained local fame by fighting the last recorded duel in Philadelphia history.

It all began when newly elected Troop Surgeon J. William White broke tradition by opting to wear a full-dress uniform instead of plain civilian clothes, as had always been the custom. As a well-known man about town (featured in Thomas Eakins' painting, *Agnew Clinic*, as the operating surgeon), White must have felt pretty confident to take such liberty. Another Trooper, the hot-headed Robert Adams, Jr. took exception to this and made White's full-dress uniform a personal crusade, complaining loudly about it whenever White was in earshot. On one such occasion, White—an accomplished Victorian pugilist—struck Adams in the face, knocking him to the floor with a single punch. Adams responded by requesting satisfaction by duel in a newspaper announcement.

According to folklore, this caused quite the stir in Philadelphia, revealing a rift in the city's collective temperament between romantics who were thrilled by that their city should still host such an anachronism and pragmatics who were appalled by it. Dueling was illegal at the time, but a few lawyers (all of them Troopers) discovered a wedge of disputed land between Pennsylvania and Delaware, falling outside Pennsylvania legal boundaries, where the confrontation could take place.

On the morning of the engagement, Adams and White faced each other and discharged their pistols following the strict 18th-century *code duello*. Both shots missed. Years later, White assured Adams that had he intentionally fired his pistol safely into the air. Adams responded by saying, "That's funny, because I aimed directly at your head."

After the duel, both men had colorful careers. White became an influential professor and trustee at the University of Pennsylvania, while Adams became United States Minister to Brazil and then a member of the U.S. House of Representatives. But Adams' temperament ultimately got the better of him. After suffering heavy losses in stock market speculation, he did to himself what he once tried with White— he shot himself in the head with a pistol.

Aside from theatrics like the dueling incident, the Troop carried on for the rest of the 19th century adhering steadily to the formula that yielded its past successes. Men who could have led other militia units chose instead to serve together in First City at low rank. After spending years as privates, they would advance to become well-grounded NCOs. According to the unit's official 1874 history, "years of association in the ranks, even before attaining Non-commissioned Grades, had become a standard requirement for promotion and resulted in unusual capability in both non-commissioned and commissioned ranks, as well as strong loyalty to the unit."

Assembling such men into one unit and asking them to adopt Rudyard Kipling's "gentleman ranker" ethos might at first glance appear to have been a misallocation of talent. But Troopers were not forced to suppress their abilities permanently. They knew that in wartime they would almost all become officers in other units—and that by having served as enlisted men, they would be the better officers for it.

The results speak for themselves. Of the nearly 3,000 men who have served in the Troop from 1774 through 2015, seventeen have attained the rank of general. To my knowledge, that is the highest number of generals to come from any single company-sized unit in the U.S. Army National Guard.

The Troop's equestrian culture certainly reinforced this esprit. Many of its members were nationally ranked horsemen. For example, Captain Fairman Rogers was among the first Americans to introduce polo to the United States from England. Troopers quickly adopted the game, competed nationally, and defeated the 6th Cavalry Lancers in the United States Army's first recognized polo tournament. They also helped form fox hunting clubs throughout the Philadelphia area whose legacies continue today. For example, the Radnor Hunt Club continues to waive fees for Active Roll Troop members.

*Cowboy illustrator, painter, and sculptor Frederick Remington made a number of prints depicting Troopers on horseback for Harpers Weekly. The illustration above is from 1888, titled "Evolutions of the First City Troop of Philadelphia, the Winner in the Cavalry Drill Contest at the New York Horse Show." (First City Troop collection)*

Like many of his peers, Rogers pursued various civilian interests. He helped found the University of Pennsylvania's Department of Mines, Arts, and Manufacturers, as well as Philadelphia's Union League—which remains one of the most well-appointed town clubs in America today. As chairman of the Building Committee for the Pennsylvania Academy of the Fine Arts, he ran the design competition that selected Frank

Furness as the architect of the school's famous main building. An avid coaching enthusiast, he authored *A Manual of Coaching*—which, oddly enough, is still considered the definitive guide to the sport. (Even more oddly, true to its passion for anachronism, the Philadelphia region remains a world center today for Four-in-Hand driving.) He also appeared in Thomas Eakins' painting *The Fairman Rogers Four-in-Hand*, the first painting to accurately display horse leg movements, as identified through systematic photographic analysis.

Until the advent of automobiles, almost everyone in the Troop lived in Center City, mainly near Rittenhouse Square. They gathered each Monday night for drill equitation at the Armory, renting horses from nearby livery stables. After drill, they would gather with their wives at each other's houses for dinner. These meals were sometimes elaborate, with eight or nine courses, each paired with carefully selected wines. With wives and children so thoroughly incorporated into weekly Troop routine, the organization enjoyed tremendous generational continuity, which was further reinforced by a general Philadelphia preoccupation with *family*. As Mark Twain once quipped (and it still applies today), "In Boston they ask, how much does he know? In New York, how much is he worth? In Philadelphia, who were his parents?"

*Five Cadwalader brothers (above) were typical of boys in the First City Troop family. They "drilled" together as children, and later served together as adults (below). (First City Troop collection)*

# Chapter 7

# The Spanish American War

In 1898, war erupted between the United States and Spain. As a militia unit, the Troop was not obligated to deploy abroad, but it registered to mobilize immediately with the United States Volunteer Service, its members answering the call from around the world. Private George C. Thayer, traveling in Russia, Corporal Sam Chew, searching for gold in the Alaskan Klondike, and Charles Wheeler (an older man, long off the Active Roll), touring Japan, all dropped what they were doing to return home to deploy with their friends.

Unprepared for the rigors awaiting them, the Troop departed from the Armory on a cold morning, slipping and splashing through slushy Philadelphia streets. Then they spent ten weeks at Camp Gretna, Pennsylvania, eating, sleeping, and training in continuous rain. In late July, they sailed for Puerto Rico on the cargo ship *Massachusetts*, in appalling conditions. According to Trooper James Cooper, 700 men and 1,400 horses and mules shared a vessel originally designed to carry 400 horses. Suffering seasickness, the men slept in hammocks jammed so tightly together that they collided with each other as the vessel pitched and tossed at sea. Animal's hooves stomped and scraped on the berths above and beneath them night and day. The "offensively fragrant" stench was overwhelming. Compounding this misery, drinking water, described as "a dirty yellowish fluid," was in dangerously short supply, causing numerous animal deaths from dehydration.

To top all that off, when the ship reached Puerto Rico, it ran aground. Troopers cheered this catharsis, greeting the emergency as a chance to improvise ways to get their equipment and surviving animals ashore—and do some swimming.

*First Lieutenant Browning, Captain Groome, and Second Lieutenant McFadden dressed for the tropics. When Troopers were issued the Army's new khaki uniforms—the same model that Rough Rider Teddy Roosevelt had run up for himself at Brooks Brothers—they much preferred the older blue-colored service dress. Although initially disliked, these uniforms would later be immortalized in the Troop's silver-candelabra engravings. (James Cooper, 1898)*

With their experience organizing hunting expeditions at home, the men brought amenities with them that surprised observers. According to a New York Sun reporter, the Troop was the only American unit to bring their own water filter, and they exhibited great pride in cooking, adding, "They shirked no duty, no matter how disagreeable...So much for the dude soldier."

*Troopers organize a makeshift "Sergeant's Club" in the field. (James Cooper, 1898)*

Before deploying, Captain Groome had specifically requested that his men be equipped with gray colored horses, which he deemed the most serviceable color for use in the tropics. The men adopted an idiosyncratic field dress in utter contrast to their penchant for dandy smartness and tribal uniformity back in Philadelphia. Outdoing one another in whimsy, each Trooper assembled his rig as he best saw fit, mixing up older blue service uniforms with bespoke silk shirts cut to regulation army patterns. Each favored his own style of boots and headdress, some having purchased straw hats from the locals. Thus attired, they slept on bare earth, wrapped in soaking blankets, sinking into mud inches deep. The surprising amount of rain they thought they had escaped in Pennsylvania now seemed dwarfed in comparison to Puerto Rico's rainy season. Cooper said, "The closest friends of the Troopers would never have recognized these rain bedraggled warriors as the same men who so often dressed so resplendently in the streets of Philadelphia as part of the Honor Guard of the President of the U.S.A. or distinguished soldiers."

*Troopers march to Cayey. (James Cooper, 1898)*

Advancing into enemy territory, the Troop came within sight of Spanish entrenchments on the road to Cayey. Expecting a fight, the First Sergeant gathered everyone and warned, "In a scrap like this, the cavalry are sure to be heavily engaged. A good many of us are bound to be stopped [killed or wounded]." In spite of their pre-combat jitters, a phlegmatic spirit ruled the moment. According to Cooper, half an hour before the attack, "The First City Troopers at this crucial moment revealed still an absolutely amazing indifference to the conflict now all but upon them—most of them were asleep." As they awaited the signal to advance, a lieutenant galloped up furiously with a dispatch ordering General Brooke (the Troop's Corps commander) to cease all operations. The United States and Spain had just agreed to end hostilities. Exasperated at this anti-climax, Captain Groome sent Lieutenant Browning to approach the commander of the Sixth Spanish Infantry Battalion in its fortified blockhouse with a request for surrender. Browning obeyed, fashioning a white flag from a finely made table linen his wife had donated to the Troop's Mess, which remains preserved in the Troop's museum collection today.

*Troopers recuperate after hostilities in Puerto Rico while waiting to return home. They had been too preoccupied with the campaign over the preceding months to notice that they all looked like skeletons from tropical rigors. (James Cooper, 1898)*

On the boat ride home (according to Cooper), Troopers were "obliged to smile" at the airs New York soldiers affected as they "boasted much of the fine reception which they felt sure was in store for them, and looked rather pityingly upon the

Philadelphia cavalrymen." As their ship passed the Statue of Liberty toward Manhattan, six flag-festooned tugboats appeared out of the mist, full of cheering civilians. Seeing these boats, the men of Gotham exclaimed, "Here comes the advance guard of our escort!" Cooper responded in silence when it soon became apartment that five of the six tugs had been commandeered by Philadelphians. The Troop's old trumpeter, Ellis Pugh, greeted his returning comrades by sounding out the familiar notes of the *First City Troop March* on the leading boat.

Once the Troopers returned home, their friends and family commissioned a handsome silver table service to commemorate the deployment—made of melted Spanish doubloons. The set included a sixty-pint-capacity punch bowl, two tall flagons, and four candelabra, each with ten lamps. The base of each candelabrum was decorated with images of soldiers dressed in the unpopular 1898 khaki field uniform. Like British cavalry regiments, the Troop sees its silver collection as a symbolic part of the unit's cultural identity today.

*Detail of the Troop's 1898 candelabra (above). (Author's photo)*
*Periodic silver polishing parties (below) are a common*
*experience for the Active Roll. (Photo by Ryan Noyes)*

# Chapter 8

# National Guard and State Police

In February 1899, within a year of the Troop's return from Puerto Rico, their drill hall collapsed under the weight of heavy snow. Damage to the walls was so extensive that the Active Roll voted to build a new Armory from scratch at 23rd and Ranstead Streets. This was a sad decision, considering the sentimental attachment already associated with the Furness-designed building. The new building, completed in 1901, remains the unit's home today. According to Troop lore (in this case rather dubious), an original Dunlap copy of the Declaration of Independence was included in a time capsule that was encased in lead beneath the building's cornerstone.

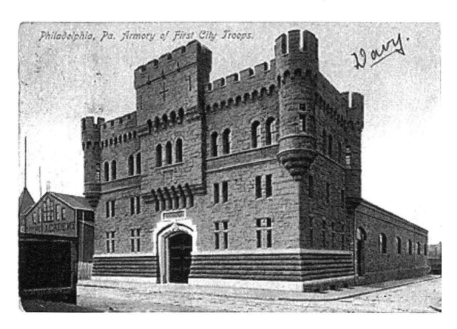

*(Previous page) The second Armory, built at 23rd and Ranstead Streets in 1901, is still the home of the First City Troop today. (The Library Company of Philadelphia)*

While Troop adjusted to its new Armory, Congress signed the Dick Act of 1903, incorporating militia units across the United States into a new entity called the National Guard. Units that had once been locally financed would now be federally funded. The United States Army would regulate them, but state governors would still they would still hold them in ultimate control.

Pre-existing militia units were able to choose whether to join this National Guard or to remain exclusively local as "state defense forces." Troopers voted to align with the National Guard. As a unit pre-dating the United States of America, the Troop was allowed to retain its distinctive uniforms, election process, and rank structure as "ancient rights and privileges" guaranteed in the Militia Act of 1792. In 1903 there were numerous "ancient" American militia units that met this qualification, but the Troop is the only one still active today.

But Troopers quickly discovered that they would have to sometimes need to fight to retain this status. In 1915, the Pennsylvania State Legislature drafted documents threatening the rights ensured by the Dick Act. In response, Active, Non-active and Honorary Troopers poured a flood of personal memoranda into Harrisburg from across the country, until the Pennsylvania Adjutant General intervened to ensure the Troop's right to its own elections, uniforms, and nomenclature.

Like many other American militia units, the Troop was mobilized throughout the 1870s, 80s, 90s, and early 1900s to suppress violent labor strikes. Guidons in the Armory's mess hall today commemorate deployments to Pittsburgh, Homestead, and Hazelton. The 1902 coal strikes in Luzerne County and Tamaqua were especially bitter, which struck a nerve among Troopers whose family money came from iron and coal. When they deployed to the coal regions, they were grieved at how unfairly some of the private company-town police treated the miners.

Troop Captain John Groome took his concerns to Pennsylvania Governor Samuel Pennypacker, who responded by asking Groome to form a new state-run constabulary to keep order in the coal regions. After a fact-finding trip in Europe, Groome returned home and established the Pennsylvania State Police, using the First City Troop as his primary model. Other states followed suit, and as a result, state police forces across the United States are called "State *Troopers*" today.

## Chapter 9

# Mexican Border and World War I

In June 1916, the Troop was sent with other National Guard units to patrol the United States-Mexican border at Fort Bliss in El Paso, Texas. The men remained there for seven months, living in the desert with cacti, coyotes, scorpions, and mesquite. They spent their first weeks breaking and "gentling" green army horses, learning their personalities, and sustaining injuries from bites, kicks and falls in the process.

*Trooper and horse navigate a pistol range in this undated photo. There was once a clever and longsuffering horse called "Lapsely Wilson," who, after getting his ears nicked by too many green, shaky marksmen, learned to "gallop in place" on the pistol range whenever he got near target—to allow his rider an easier shot. (First City Troop collection)*

*George Brooke stands on the Mexican Border with "Persimmon," the U.S. Army horse he trained and broke himself. (George Brooke, 1917)*

In his book, *With the First City Troop on the Mexican Border*, George Brooke described how the Army hired a professional bronco buster to help with especially difficult horses. Troopers were amazed at the skill of an African American who easily tamed "outlaw" horses that other soldiers couldn't touch. "Chuck full of confidence," his trick was to approach horses with calmness, self-command, and great strength, "always applied at the right time and in the right place."

*Troopers devour newspapers from home. (George Brooke, 1917)*

Brooke described a slew of military constants that later Troopers would experience on deployments in the Middle East. For example, citing the enlisted man's timeless compulsion to speculate about events he knows knowing about, Brooke wrote, "The rumor squad is hard at work these days. First you hear that we are to parade in Washington on Labor Day and then that an invasion of Mexico is planned for the 15th of October." He described the monotony that Troopers experienced who were accustomed to busy professional lives back home, citing one officer who worried that he was losing his mind. And he captured the constant, underlying hilarity of Troopers mocking themselves as "smart men doing dumb things," an ongoing joke that remains unchanged today. Like that time when his friend's horse decided to lay down while crossing a stream, and then, after finally being led out, rolled on all his equipment. Brooke chuckled, "You can't help having an amusing incident when the sixth squad are all present and accounted for."

*On the Mexican Border, Troopers formed polo teams. The team of Ingersoll, Randolph, Converse, and McFadden (above) completed with General Pershing's team at Fort Bliss. In addition to playing polo, Troopers established a steeple chase competition called the Border Plate, which is still held annually. (George Brooke, 1917)*

Not long after the Troop returned home from Texas, the United States entered World War I on the side of Britain and France. Anticipating another deployment, Captain George Thayer gathered the entire Active Roll and encouraged them to immediately seek commissions Reserve Officers. Jack Borland Thayer Jr. and Percy Childs Madeira, Jr. were among the Troopers who took his advice.

They both led active lives. At age 17, Thayer was one of the few people to survive the sinking of the Titanic by jumping overboard into the sea. Much shaken by the incident, he suffered psychologically from it for the rest of his life. He deployed with the Troop to Texas in 1916, became an officer after returning home, and then led an artillery company in France the next year. Later he would chair the Haverford

School's Board of Directors and serve as a University of Pennsylvania treasurer and trustee. During World War II, he lost his eldest son Edward, the first Trooper killed in that war. Madeira, who also served on the Mexican Border as an enlisted man, fought as a captain during World War I as well. As a civilian, he became a respected Philadelphia lawyer and banker and later an archeologist, participating in a landmark 1930 expedition that photographed Yucatán and Guatemalan ruins from the air. Like Thayer, Madeira also ended his career with the University of Pennsylvania—in this case, as its Museum of Archeology chairman.

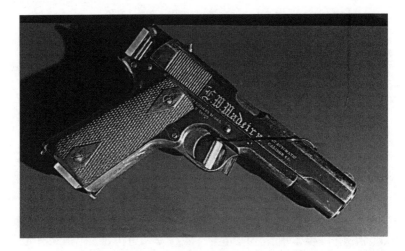

*Percy Childs Madeira's privately purchased and engraved service pistol, on display at the Armory's museum. (Author's photo)*

Because so many Troopers left the Active Roll on Thayer's advice, he had to recruit a fresh new unit from scratch. He did this quickly by tapping brothers, relatives, and friends of the older members. The majority of these men were well below draft age and under no obligation to join the military.

In order to select NCOs from these raw recruits (gentleman-rankers all), he struck upon a novel idea: to give each man a chance at leadership, he appointed six acting corporals from among them to serve for a short time period, and then rotated this line-up until everyone in the unit had a chance to boss around his peers. After seeing how they all behaved, he selected permanent NCOs by common consent.

In September, Thayer learned that the Army would not be using horse cavalry in France. This news caused uproar! Extended Troop family members were so appalled that they hired prominent Philadelphia lawyer Michael Francis Doyle to argue a case against the United States Army to carve out a role for horses solely for the First City Troop. Philadelphia newspapers followed the story, posting daily articles about the Troop's fight to preserve its identity as a horse unit.

The outcry reached comical proportions when Philadelphia social grandees attempted to throw their weight around in Washington, assuming their provincial importance was influential at the national level. The Secretary of War received nasty telegrams from the Daughters of the American Revolution, the Society of the Cincinnati, Senator Boies Penrose, Governor Martin G. Brumbaugh, and others. The campaign peaked when J. Willis Martin sent the following missive representing the primordial Schuylkill Fishing Company to the Secretary of War in October 1917:

*"As governor of the oldest social organization in the United States, organized in 1732, and from which the First Troop Philadelphia City Calvary was recruited, I request that in consideration of the active services of the Troop in the Revolution, War of 1812, Mexican War, Civil War, War with Spain, and its continued existence*

*as a troop of cavalry since its organization in 1774, prior to the formation of the United States Army, that an order be issued permitting its identity to be retained during the present war. Sincerely, J. Willis Martin, Governor State in Schuylkill."*

Wondering perhaps what on earth the State in Schuylkill was, the Secretary of War made no recorded response to Martin's communication attempt.

As Old Philadelphian appeals fell on deaf ears, the Troop was assigned to headquarters duty with the 28th Infantry Division—a role which heaped insult upon injury. Facing mundane administrative tasks like clerical work, mule driving, and blacksmithing, drove the men toward revolt. The Troop celebrated its 143rd Anniversary Dinner on November 17, 1916 in sad spirits indeed. Temporarily absorbed into Company E of the 103rd Engineers, they wondered if their organizational history had finally come to an end.

Just when all seemed lost, the Pennsylvania Adjutant General—a longtime Troop ally—personally intervened, instructing the 28th Infantry Division commander to find a combat role for the Troop. The only spot available was in the 103rd Trench Mortar Battery. This offered little chance for panache, but at it was a combat role that would allow the Active Roll to deploy under the Troop Standard. The unit's honor was thus saved.

After five months of training, Troopers sailed to France on the lyrically named transport ship *Saturnia*. Conditions on the front were harsh. According to historian Paul Fusell, a "stench of rotten flesh was over everything; hardly repressed by the chloride of lime sprinkled on particularly offensive sites…you could smell the front line before you could see it." During the Argonne offensive, two Troop gun crews were hit while advancing toward German lines, costing twelve lives. The unit later attacked an entrenched German position at Le Chene Tondu Ridge, which had earlier been holding up the American advance. The Troop moved briefly to Verdun and then to Ypres, where it served with the rest of the 28th Infantry Division in pursuit of the retreating German army.

No reference to World War I is complete without mentioning a promising young man cut down in the bloom of youth. The most notable example in the Troop was Harry McKean Ingersoll. An artillery officer who had earlier deployed with the Troop on the Mexican border, Ingersoll was a classic Edwardian all-rounder—the sort of talented, charming, and unpretentious gentleman celebrated in British literature at the time. From the Western Front, he wrote letters to his mother in Bar Harbor, cheerfully describing massive rats, calf-deep mud, and copious body lice. On September 25, 1918, his final letter began, "Dear Mama, tomorrow we start the great battle. Just a line to let you know that I go into it full of hope and confidence in myself, to see it through. . . ." The next letter preserved in the family archives, dated October 3, 1918, began, "My Dear Mrs. Ingersoll, if I could only tell you how it breaks my heart to write you this letter. . ."

Ingersoll was shot twice—once in the neck and once above the hip, where the bullet exited the upper thigh. The second bullet, which severed the femoral artery, was the one that proved fatal. Having died while leading an attack on enemy positions which had hitherto delayed American advances in that sector, he was posthumously awarded the

Distinguished Service Cross. His hat, pipe, and other personal effects are currently displayed in the Troop's museum.

*Harry Ingersoll. (First City Troop collection)*

Throughout World War I, 242 Troop members served in uniform, and 183 of these were officers. The unit suffered fifteen casualties. Based on this showing, a Troop historian just after the war concluded:

> *"In supplying the government with so many officers, the Troop accomplished its ideal of service. While deprived of the opportunity of serving with the Troop in the war, these Troopers rendered greater service to the nation than they could have done as enlisted men and the ranks of their original organization."*

The war reinforced the idea that the Troop must serve a dual purpose—to be both an active National Guard combat unit, capable of fighting in its own right, and a leadership school, a training ground for future officers.

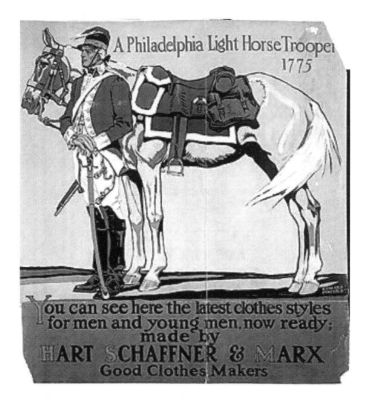

*Troop was famous enough in World War I for Hart, Schaffner & Marx to use them in advertising. (Poster donated to Troop by Honorary Captain Henry Ingersoll and David "Rat" Smith)*

*Like other Troopers of his era, Colonel Robert Edward Glendinning (photo above) was quite the accomplished all-rounder. While attending the University of Pennsylvania in the 1880s, he modeled nude for Eadweard Muybridge's landmark photographic study, "Animal Locomotion." He deployed with the Troop during the Spanish American War, took over the family bank, Robert Glendinning & Co. (photo below) when he returned home, and became the first Governor of the New York Stock Exchange from outside New York. He helped pioneer seaplane technology at the Aero Club of Pennsylvania (photo below), commanded the American air forces in Italy during World War I, and received high decorations from the Italian king and from the United States government. A devoted local volunteer, he helped found Chestnut Hill Hospital and Philadelphia School for the Deaf, and he served as treasurer of the Fairmount Park Commission and director of the Philadelphia Zoological Society. (First City Troop collection)*

## Chapter 10

# Interwar in Arcadia

In 1922, General John J. Pershing visited the Armory with Major George C. Marshall (the future Army Chief of Staff during World War II) to commemorate George Washington's birthday. Impressed to see so many young men "of practically independent fortune" training for military readiness, Pershing later wrote: "No national guard organization in the country did more relatively in the War than the 1st troop Philadelphia City Cavalry." In response to this pleasing—if somewhat qualified—statement, Pershing was soon elected to the Honorary Roll.

*General Pershing inspects First City in 1922 with future Army Chief of Staff George Marshall in tow. Pershing soon became an honorary Trooper himself. (First City Troop collection)*

Equine sports remained popular after World War I. By the 1920's, First City Troopers whose grandfathers had once lived in Philadelphia's Rittenhouse section had migrated into beautiful, insular suburban enclaves toward Germantown, Chestnut Hill, and the Main Line, where they could keep their own horses. These rural neighborhoods characterized a uniquely Philadelphian form of 18th-century-inspired high living that would appear in regional literature for decades to come.

*Troopers compete in the 1924 Border Plate, an annual steeplechase competition which began in 1916 on the Mexican border and continues today. Once held at the Whitemarsh Valley Hunt Club, a lovely fox-hunting place later obliterated by the Pennsylvania Turnpike, the Border Plate has been held at various locations over the years, moving inexorably as Philadelphia horse country's center of gravity shifts in response to ever-expanding exurbia. (Troop History, 1874-1948)*

According to Nathaniel Burt's *The Perennial Philadelphians* and Richard Powell's *The Philadelphian*, two books that remain a local classics, the Philadelphia gentry created a "modern Arcadia" of remodeled stone farmhouses, large enough for dignity but small enough for modesty, surrounded by pastures and post-and-rail fences. Powell explained that in the late 1920s, people from the Troop's social demographic sought updated houses that looked as if their families had lived in them for generations. Because nobody could pretend that English castles, French chalets, or Italian villas had been around Philadelphia for very long, "architects came up with the Pennsylvania farmhouse... a low rambling structure of fieldstone and clapboard, which always succeeded in giving the impression that Washington had slept there."

Grasping for ways to describe how this unique variant of the American way of life blended a range of traits seemingly at odds everywhere else, Burt said, "The quality of Philadelphia buildings and furnishings and silver somewhat resembles the quality of Philadelphia food: rich and smooth, as in creamed oysters, chicken or seafood croquettes, White Mountain cake and Philadelphia ice cream." Furniture followed English models "with sumptuous fidelity, always a few decades behind the times...simpler and less elaborate than its models, less virtuoso, less creative, [giving] an effect of better taste in being less showy and ornate and pompous."

Many Troop families settled near Penllyn, an area outside Chestnut Hill especially blessed with turnpike taverns and remodeled farmhouses of colonial vintage. In *Philadelphia Gentlemen*, E. Digby Baltzell described Penllyn as an "almost studied atmosphere of old money" where people with hobby farms lived in "hard-riding simplicity," far from the formal estates and manicured lawns on the Main Line. Along crooked, tree-shaded lanes, lined with wide bridle paths, they created the illusion that they were really just plain old country folk after all—within just a few miles of the factories and smokestacks of the industrial civilization that supported them. On farms owned by the oldest Troop families, children were raised to be yeomen as well as country squires, bailing hay and mucking stables alongside the hired hands. According to Cordelia Drexel Biddle, some Philadelphians intentionally carried this rural sensibility along with them on their semi-annual visits to New York City, where they would wear tweeds instead of dress suits, "to show their disdain for the parvenus and upstarts in Manhattan."

In the summer of 1937, Captain John Groome, Jr. led the Troop through another section of Philadelphia's alluring horse country when he and his men chose to return to Philadelphia from summer camp at Indiantown Gap on horseback instead of by rail. The 110-mile march, conducted in a heat wave that reached 115 degrees, was referenced in numerous Philadelphia newspapers.

Although forced to ride all night through Lancaster County because anti-military Amish farm-owners would not allow them to bivouac, in Chester County they received a much better welcome. After pausing to cool off in a swimming pool at Corporal John Kent Kane's estate, Shirely Farms, they bivouacked at Sergeant William Ashton's Delchester Farms. Ashton hosted the entire unit to dinner, including many Troopers' wives, who had been invited to join them informally.

To keep things militarily authentic (they were on duty after all), the men bivouacked on one of Ashton's fields where they got thoroughly soaked in a hard rain overnight. Upon arrival in Philadelphia the next day, Troop members of the Honorary and Non-active Rolls greeted them with a lavish brunch called a Hughie's Breakfast, which was (and remains) the customary way for the Troop to end annual training. Their ride stands in local history as the longest cavalry march in Pennsylvania since the Civil War.

Around this time—as always—Troopers were dabbling in all sorts of things outside their professional occupations and military service. For example, Henry Sandwith Drinker, Jr. was a Philadelphia lawyer who spent all his spare time playing music and translating Bach, Schubert, Haydn's vocal works from German into English. He and his wife would host nearly a hundred people at their home on Sunday nights for massive classical sing-along dinners. In 1938, Drinker discovered a European family called the von Trapps, who sang magnificently and wanted to immigrate to the United States following the Nazi annexation of Austria. Drinker helped them get visas at Ellis Island and then set them up in a handsome Main Line house at 252 Merion Road. For a while, they roamed around wearing Tyrolean dirndls and lederhosen because they couldn't afford other clothes. These soon became their trademark when they started touring as the Trapp Family Singers. Broadway composers Rodgers and Hammerstein took a shine to them, and eventually turned their story into a musical called *The Sound of Music*, which would win five Oscars in 1965.

On September 11, 1939, Captain John Groome assembled the Active Roll to discuss Germany's invasion of Poland and England's decision to declare war. Like Captain Thayer a generation earlier, Groome suggested that each man immediately take a correspondence course to become a second lieutenant. Following his advice, sixty five out of seventy enlisted Troopers became officers. Among those men was Trooper Nicholas Wainwright, who would later become a prominent Philadelphia historian. Horrified to think that the Troop's bawdy song book might fall into unfriendly hands and embarrass his and his friends' families if they should die in the coming war, he crept into the Armory's silver vault (where the book was kept) and stole it for safekeeping for the duration.

*Troopers practice a "pistol charge" at annual training in 1941. Such tactics would have had minimal wartime utility. When the Polish cavalry tried them against the Wehrmacht two years earlier, they proved suicidal. (First City Troop collection)*

# Chapter 11

# World War II

In early 1942, the National Guard changed its policy about horses and decided to stop using them entirely. This crushed Troopers' morale because the men deeply loved their steeds. (To imagine how attached they were to their horses, a modern male might imagine the affection he would have if his favorite dog were combined with his favorite car or motorcycle.) The 28th Division Pennsylvania National Guard announced their decision to take away the horses while the Troopers' regiment was training in Virginia.

And so it came to pass that on April 2nd, 1942, during a heavy downpour, the horse vans moved out of Front Royal, while the regimental band played *The Old Gray Mare* over and over. But the day was not without comic relief. The Stable Sergeant tried to conceal his mount in a room on the second floor of the barracks, and another Trooper he had to be hospitalized when he attempted to kiss his horse goodbye and the horse nearly bit off his nose.

Troop's first wartime area of responsibility stretched along the Delaware River industrial area from Port Richmond to Marcus Hook and included all electrical power and transmission plants, regardless of location. The port of Philadelphia received trainloads of war materiel daily. It arrived in such a volume that guns, ammunition, tanks, trucks, tires, and brand new railroad locomotives sprawled out over acres, with no barbed wire to protect them.

Suffering a constant manpower drain as higher command cherry picked senior privates and NCOs for officer training (in 1942 alone, personnel turnover exceeded 100 percent), Troop Captain Henry Coxe, Jr. maintained cultural hegemony within the Active Roll by taking new members on marches through Revolutionary War sites where the Troop had served, using the unit's own historical records to describe each engagement. Contemporary accounts suggest that this program had a profound effect on new members.

In 1943, the Troop was sent to Salem, Oregon, to defend the coast against Japanese incursion. In early 1944, they decamped to Los Angeles where they engaged in such operations as patrolling the Malibu beach and investigating incidences of suspected sabotage. One suspects that these duties were minimally taxing. Within months, they went to Camp Polk, Louisiana for intensive combat training, and were finally sent Europe in 1945, well after the 28th Infantry Division Guard sustained its appalling casualties at Hürtgen Forest. After Germany surrendered, they were sent to the Philippines to prepare for invading Japan, an operation that United States military planners expected to cost up to 1,000,000 American casualties. Happily, Japan surrendered while their ship was making a stop in New York City.

On December 16th, 1945, the extended Troop family gathered at the annual George Washington Memorial church service to thank God for victory and mourn the lost and injured. As the Color Guard led Active Roll Troopers into St. Peter's Church, Troopers from duty stations around the world marched behind them, wearing the uniforms of their most recent service branches. It was an emotionally powerful homecoming.

William Williams Keen Butcher, Crawford Clark Madeira, and Adolph Rosengarten are three men (drawn at random) whose military records demonstrate how far afield Troopers served.

Butcher left the Active Roll at the war's outbreak to commission with the 34th Infantry Division, which served 517 straight days of combat in Italy—the longest action by any American division in any of the nation's wars. Madeira left the Active Roll to serve as a United States liaison officer with the Chinese Army on the Burma Road. Rosengarten found his way into a Military Intelligence unit assigned to the top-secret Ultra group, which decoded German messages at Bletchley Park in England. During the Normandy invasion, he was the first Ultra officer to cross the English Channel. All three of these men had been privates when serving in the Troop before the war.

In later life, Butcher helped build the bond-trading firm Butcher & Singer into one of Philadelphia's most profitable companies, and remained a devoted First City Trooper until death. Madeira worked in Brussels as European marketing director for the agricultural conglomerate Monsanto. After retiring from business, he spent his time as a Lankenau Hospital volunteer, driving a truck for the Meals on Wheels program. Rosengarten achieved national prominence for the gardens at Chanticleer, his family's country house in Wayne, Pennsylvania. (The house had been built decades earlier by Zantzinger, Borie, and Medary, a Trooper-owned architectural firm which designed gothic residence halls at Princeton University.) As an older man, Rosengarten was shot in the chest point blank while struggling with an armed burglar who entered his house. Made of stern stuff, he survived the wound and kept the extracted bullet on his watch chain for the rest of his life as a keepsake.

Of the 255 Troopers who served in WWII, 206 were officers. Ten were killed in action. Among the officers were one Brigadier General, nine Colonels, twenty four Lieutenant Colonels, thirty five Majors, eighty three Captains, and thirty eight First Lieutenants in the Army; one Lieutenant Colonel and two Majors in the Marine Corps; two Captains, nine Commanders, twelve Lieutenant Commanders, seven Lieutenants, and one Lieutenant Junior Grade in the Navy; and one Commander in the Coast Guard.

*All Rolls celebrate the Troop's 175th anniversary in 1949, with Mexican Border veterans seated at the table in the foreground. There were so many attendees that year, that a tent was erected in the drill hall to accommodate them all. (First City Troop Collection)*

*Barclay Harding Warburton sits with his buddies at the 175ᵗʰ anniversary dinner. Born in 1866, he inherited the Philadelphia Evening Telegraph newspaper from his father, served with the Troop in the Spanish American War, married into the rich Wanamaker family, and like many Troopers, left the Active Roll to lead another unit. He received the British Distinguished Service Order and the French Legion of Honor in World War I as an artillery officer. In the 1920s, he served as director of welfare and special police commissioner (unpaid mayor-appointed positions) for the city of Philadelphia, and also as one-time mayor of (where else?) Palm Beach. A local grandee, his house in Palm Beach was palatial. (First City Troop collection)*

# Chapter 12

# A New Cavalry Role

After World War II, the Troop faced the question of whether it would remain a cavalry unit in the Pennsylvania National Guard or become an officer training cadre for the Army Reserve. All Rolls unanimously vetoed the latter option, believing that Troopers benefited more by serving as enlisted men than they would as officers. They feared that if the unit were an officer training cadre, individuals would become too concerned with their own careers, and there would be "too many chiefs and not enough Indians."

*Troopers await departure for officer training in 1950. (Troop History: 1948-1991)*

87

A 1946 circular insisted that although every effort would be made to encourage Troopers to qualify as officers in the event of war, the Troop would lose its mystique, egalitarianism, and esprit de corps if it became a professional school for officers. "The Troop's future must be based, as it always has been in the past, on comradeship... it cannot long endure on the basis of every man for himself."

After conferring with National Guard Bureau and War Department chiefs of staff, and with the 28th Infantry Division's commander, Troop Captain Robert Norton Downs arranged for the Troop to serve as the division commander's personal reconnaissance unit. This was an ideal mission. The only hitch was that the Troop would have to expand its roster and become much larger than it had been in the past, forcing it to be less selective about admitting new prospects to the Active Roll.

By accepting its new role in the 28th Infantry Division, the Troop had to comply with the United States Army's age standards for officers. Until then, captains in the Troop were often as old as Brigadiers in the regular army, having served decades in the unit before getting promoted. That custom would now have to change. In one year, Captain Downs, First Lieutenant Thayer, Second Lieutenant Frazier, and Cornet Ashton all resigned, and a new group of relative youngsters was elected in their place.

*Newly mechanized Troopers leave the Armory for annual training at Indiantown Gap in 1950. (From the Philadelphia Evening Bulletin Photograph Collection. Courtesy of the Special Collections Research Center, Temple University Libraries. Philadelphia, PA 19122)*

When post-war Pennsylvania National Guard training resumed in 1947, a brief golden age flourished as Troopers lectured each other on lessons gleaned from World War II. Wearing civilian clothes and ignoring references to military rank, they conducted theoretical reconnaissance problems with scales models on a sand table in the riding hall. At Annual Training at Fort Indiantown Gap, they ran their own training schedule, borrowing Jeeps, radios, blank ammunition, and smoke grenades to stage all-day reconnaissance scenarios. Midway through training, they bivouacked at a local farm, and around a large bonfire, composed new bawdy songs to dramatize significant mishaps from the prior year.

89

# Chapter 13

# Deployment to Germany

Peacetime didn't last long. War broke out in Korea in 1950. The Troop was federalized the following September, and were sent to Camp Atterbury, Indiana to train for a deployment to Germany the following year.

Because this mobilization came so close on the heels of the last war, the Troop had difficulty filling its roster. So, for the first time since the Civil War, they resorted to public advertising to fill spots that could not be met by existing members' friends and family.

The Troop's new captain, William Stanley Stokes, helped ease this transition by setting a strong example in looks, efficiency, and personal behavior. Bright, capable, and (according to some) so polite as to seem almost Victorian, he would eventually rise to the rank of general. He had a 1930s Hollywood, Errol Flynn, look about him. While speaking with locals in the late 1950s to research his book *Perennial Philadelphians*, Nathaniel Burt heard Stokes described as "the Handsomest Man ever Seen." Like other Troopers before him, Stokes counterbalanced his perfectionist streak by cultivating some eccentric quirks. For example, he was rumored to mow his lawn with a flame thrower. Referring to this legend, a Trooper who joined the unit in the 1980s said, "I always thought it was myth until I bumped into his widow—a force of nature herself—at a party, who confirmed that this was indeed his preferred landscaping technique!"

*The dashing William Stanley Stokes featured in a newspaper article (above) and seated second from right at Troop anniversary dinner (below). (First City Troop collection)*

John Walton, whose father deployed to France with the Troop during World War I, joined the unit just in time for its 1950 mobilization. As he recalled, "At Camp Atterbury, we became a cadre unit. That is, training draftees who were then sent to Korea." To Walton's fascination, Captain Stokes struck upon a unique method for cherry-picking what he thought were the best draftees passing through Camp Atterbury. "For whatever reason," said Walton, "Stokes believed that Ohio produced the best army recruits of any state in the union. I have no idea why he would expect Ohio—of all places—to produce the best men, but he was adamant. He wouldn't consider anyone from any other state! Perhaps he idealized Ohioans as hardworking but well-educated farm boys." Therefore, whenever a new group of draftees came along, Stokes would go to the orderly room, thumb through all the files, and earmark the name of anyone from Ohio.

*(Previous page) Troop marches past Philadelphia's 30th Street Station before deploying to Germany in 1951. (Troop History: 1948-1991)*

Before shipping off to Germany from New York City, Walton and his friend Jim Wallace found themselves in an embarrassing predicament. Wallace's uncle, Nelson Rockefeller, had invited them to a dinner he was hosting for the United States ambassador to Switzerland. Having been asked to attend at the last minute, the young Troopers showed up with the clothes on their backs— the "grubby and ill-fitting" World War II surplus fatigues they had been wearing at Camp Atterbury. Shrugging their shoulders, they sat down to eat acting as if their collective appearance were the most natural thing in the world. To their surprise, the ambassador's daughter took a shine to Wallace and invited both Troopers to visit her in Switzerland later that year.

*Troopers training for deployment in 1951 wearing their "grubby and ill fitting" fatigue uniforms, left over from World War II. (Troop History: 1948-1991)*

93

When they reached Bavaria, the men where happily ushered into well-appointed barracks that had originally been built for the Luftwaffe. Captain Stokes lived nearby with his family, whom he brought along for the year. Stokes' son, David, who was six years old at the time, recalls playing at the brewery across the street from his parent's house. He said, "The friendly plant workers would place me in a beer crate and then slide it on the conveyor rollers throughout the brewery like a roller coaster. The conveyor then dumped the crate, with me in it, into the back of a waiting delivery truck. The drivers would then let me sit up front with them as they made their delivery rounds through town. After an hour or so, they'd bring me safely home to mom. Can you imagine a kid being allowed to do that today?"

Throughout their time in Germany, the men spent duty hours rehearsing battle drills in preparation for Soviet attack, which at that point in the Cold War, was a very real threat. Walton recalled that they would often be awakened in the middle of the night and forced to run on full alert to guard an Autobahn bridge spanning the Danube River. His platoon's standing orders were to either defend the bridge or blow it up if the Soviets attacked.

*Maneuvers in Bavaria, 1952 (Troop History: 1948-1991)*

Over the course of the year in Bavaria, one Trooper, Theodore Voorhees Gilbert, befriended a German whose amateur aviation club had just built a homemade airplane. This was dodgy business, because at that point in post-war Germany, it was still illegal for Germans to aviate. One day, the man furtively approached Gilbert and asked if he could wrangle up a United States Army officer to attend their airplane launch, in order to give his implied blessing. Gilbert said, "Sure!" But he was unable to find an officer willing to break the law.

Unwilling to disappoint his friend—and unfazed by the law—Gilbert showed up for the airplane launch dressed as a lieutenant. (His actual rank was *corporal.*) As the homemade aircraft gathered speed on the runway and took off from the field, "Lieutenant" Gilbert stepped forward and snapped a salute, noticing only too late that a hidden film crew had just recorded the whole event. For the next few weeks, images of the launch appeared on German newsreels and newspapers with great fanfare.

When Gilbert saw the film, he noticed to his horror that everyone's face had been blocked out—except his—which made his own clearly visible face all the more prominent! Terrified of getting arrested for impersonating an officer, the normally flamboyant Gilbert spent the next weeks mincing around quietly until his enlistment expired. At his funeral sixty years later, a video of the German newsreel was proudly shown at the Armory to enthusiastic applause. Honorary First Sergeant Richard Walkup is in possession of that video today.

# Chapter 14

# The Cold War Draft

The Troop returned home from Bavaria faced with more recruiting problems. Captain Stokes addressed these by demanding that each man seeking to leave the Active Roll must find someone suitable to take his place before he could leave. Charlie Barclay enlisted in 1954 as a result of this requirement. No stranger to the organization (with forebears serving in the Troop off and on since the Revolution), Barclay was sort of shanghaied into it. As he recalled, "My sister's friend was dating a Trooper. He discovered me, and then hustled me in to take his spot, so he could get out with a clear conscience."

Other Troopers, enthusiastic to keep the unit going at all costs, availed themselves of any means to fill the Active Roll. Clarence Rich Diffenderfer, a regular Army officer who nursed a low opinion of the National Guard, joined the ranks through this less conventional route. As he put it, "I thought people only joined the Guard to avoid getting their asses shot off in the *real* Army." When I asked what sort of arduous service he performed in the "real" Army, he replied, "I served in post-war Japan as a young lieutenant. Had my own house, my own Jeep, and a beautiful 19-year-old live-in maid who had been trained all her life to look after the needs of men." Upon mentioning this last bit over the phone, Diffenderfer's voice trailed off, and for a moment, I thought I'd lost him. "Are you there?" I asked. He rejoined, "Damn, those were the best two years of my life!"

Diffenderfer went on to explain that his introduction to the National Guard followed a brusque "courtship" during the course of an evening at the Armory. While deep in their cups as guests at a Troop dinner, he and his friend John Lawson found enlistment papers placed in front of them, which they both signed. In a tone of mock offense, Diffenderfer said, "I went to sleep a lieutenant that night, and woke the next morning a *private*. Those bastards got me into the Troop like a press gang in the Royal Navy!"

President Eisenhower helped solve the Troop's recruitment problem when he signed the Reserve Forces Act of 1955 into law, which renewed the draft. Stokes' manpower problems evaporated with a stroke of Eisenhower's pen. The act included a draft deferment program, managed by Lewis B. Hershey, which aimed to channel educated young men away from combat duties and into areas deemed more useful to the state. Hershey apparently hoped that through this option he could mitigate the custom throughout American history in which the nation's "best and brightest" would rush to the colors in wartime, often becoming the first casualties.

Peter Clauss became a Trooper as a result of Hershey's program. Facing draft just as he finished Yale Law School in 1958, he assumed he should try to become an Army lawyer. But a senior partner in his law firm happened to be an Honorary Trooper, and he encouraged Clauss to visit the Armory for dinner. Clauss went to dinner, liked what he saw, and joined the unit with a new wave of young men who would eventually become his best friends.

With this new generation of college graduates starting six-year military enlistments, the Troop became one of the rare combat units in the United States (if not the only one) to have prep-school old boys and Ivy Leaguers as privates. Had it not been for the Troop, men like Clauss would likely have received officer commissions and drifted into rarified military jobs—just as Hershey intended. But in doing so, they would have forfeited the priceless learning experience that came from doing the hands-on grunt work common to all enlistees.

Recalling his exposure to the broad spectrum of recruits he met at Fort Knox while training to become a cavalry scout, Clauss said, "In the bunk next to me was Larry Christmas, whose father was a general. In the bunk above me was Coley, a convicted getaway driver in a bank heist, who was given the choice of the Army or jail because he was only 17 at the time."

Barclay and Clauss each admitted that when they joined the Troop, Monday evening drills were quite easy. Until the late 1950s, all National Guard units drilled on the same weekly schedule that militia units originated in colonial times. (To concentrate resources, they would soon switch to the monthly drill cycle that continues today.) Clauss found that solving field problems as a scout and learning to ride horses in the Troop's new equestrian program counterbalanced the long office hours he spent as a mergers and acquisitions lawyer.

Each Monday night, Barclay and his comrades would trek across the Schuylkill River to the Armory from St. Anthony Hall and Saint Elmo Club, their University of Pennsylvania fraternities. He said, "Like clockwork, drill started with cocktails at 6 p.m., followed by dinner upstairs in the mess hall. At 7:30 p.m., we would have formation and then drill until 9 p.m. We did a lot of close-order drilling with the M1 rifle. We spent the rest of the time in the classroom, where we covered topics like scouting, map reading, and how to use various types of equipment." Although training was leisurely by modern standards, Captain Stokes cracked a firm whip. He would punish rebellious Troopers by taking them out for long runs until they dropped.

While most young men commuted to drill from colleges and universities in the Philadelphia, some traveled great distances. William Rawle, for example, an athletic lad who performed a back flip off the stage at his college graduation, was training for the United States Olympic Ski Team in Vermont when he joined the Troop. Each Monday, he would drive from Vermont to Pennsylvania to meet his weekly training requirement.

Why would people like Rawle drive such distances to drill with the Troop when they could have joined another unit closer to home? Because the Troop was full of fascinating, colorful, and entertaining personalities. As one man exclaimed, "There were so many characters, and they egged each other on so much, that you didn't want to miss a single minute of drill!" Peter Clauss recalled a Troop sergeant to whom he was assigned as a driver. The sergeant, an eccentric and wealthy Main Liner, would habitually jam a brass rifle cartridge on the end of a stick, which he then carried around under his arm like a British officer's swagger stick. As Clauss drove this man around camp, the sergeant would sit in the back of the Jeep as if being chauffeured. When they came to an intersection, he would lean forward and bash Clauss on the helmet with his swagger stick to indicate which way to turn—one bash for left and two for right.

On drill nights and at summer camps, the Troop's officers and NCOs augmented National Guard training standards with their own improvements. For example, platoon leader Charlie Meredith (a former Eagle Scout) realized that

Boy Scout merit badge pamphlets offered clearer instructions for land navigation than army-issue manuals. So he bought a stack of them for his men, who used them to score superior ratings in navigation.

Meredith explained, "We were a real Cracker Jack unit because we always sought ways to improve things with our own ingenuity. It was really fun to carve out excellence that way. Naturally, we also assumed that the more often we got superior training ratings, the more of a buffer we'd have for unavoidable screw ups!"

With over a hundred men attending drill each week, there was never enough work to occupy everyone all at once. And those tasks could often be dispensed with in a fraction of the officially allotted time. After getting the men through such routine training subjects as "How to start a Jeep," "How to fix a flat tire," or "How to tie a tourniquet," the NCOs would allow the men to enjoy cocktails.

On festive occasions, they consumed drinks more exuberantly by "swinging the bucket," a venerable Troop drinking practice that may date back to the Revolutionary War, and which continues today. To do this, you tie a horse-feed bucket to an overhanging tree branch or to a building rafter, fill it with whatever beverages come to hand, and then swing it around in a circle. Participants grab the bucket while it is in swing, and then take a swig while everyone else shouts "One-Philadelphia! Two-Philadelphia! Three-Philadelphia!" Each man gets his turn. Whoever spills anything has to drink extra.

*"Swinging the Bucket" Bucket in bottom left corner. (Troop History: 1948-1991)*

As might be expected, swinging the bucket could lead to bad hangovers the next morning at first formation. In the late 1950s, two resourceful Troopers working as pharmaceutical sales reps at Smith, Kline & French discovered that pills they sold to relieve menstrual cramps worked perfectly for curing hangovers. They started dispensing these "little yellow pills" to their fellow Troopers with astonishing results. For a two- or three-year time window, the lads could stay up as late as they wanted at barracks parties and then spring out of bed fresh-faced at dawn with help from these pills. It was too good to last however. The product was yanked from the market when it was linked to vehicular accidents.

# Chapter 15

# Renewing the Equestrian Tradition

With the Troop's recruiting issues resolved, its members now considered how to maintain their equestrian tradition in a horseless cavalry age. Charlie Davis, who joined the unit in 1954, said, "My dad and uncle served in the Troop before the war—before the unit mechanized. Their routine back then was to ride at Radnor Hunt Club during the week and practice equitation each Monday night at the Armory. It deeply saddened his generation when the Army switched from horses to Jeeps. When they paved over the tanbark floor in the ring, my dad grieved over how much the smell of the building had changed!"

Like Britain's Household Cavalry, the Troop kept its equestrian culture alive by adopting a dual role as a combat unit and ceremonial unit. Each man attended weekly riding lessons in addition to modern military drill. On formal occasions, the whole Troop would ride through Center City Philadelphia on horses borrowed from the Philadelphia Police Department. In addition to equitation, the men continued to practice the same cavalry skills that Fredrick Remington observed their predecessors performing generations before. This training bore surprising fruit. Decades later, when the United States Equestrian team sought to field an American tent-pegging team (tent-pegging is an old cavalry competition) for tournaments in South Africa and India, the Troop was chosen as its representative.

*Troopers compete at tent-pegging in India. (Photo from Richard Walkup)*

A major side benefit from the Troop's post-war riding program was the way in which it built esprit de corps by forcing members to brave regular physical danger together. One man who dismissed National Guard combat training as a "joke" recalled the trepidation with which he approached his weekly riding lessons. One night he had to drive home to his wife from riding practice at Valley Forge Military Academy with a bloody face, broken glasses, and a fractured wrist sustained when his horse tossed him in close order drill at the gallop. But Troopers made light of such incidents. When a sergeant fell off his horse at the Armory one night, the men jokingly drew a chalk line around his body on the drill floor before taking him to the hospital.

*Riding lessons at Valley Forge Military Academy in 1959. (From the Philadelphia Evening Bulletin Photograph Collection. Courtesy of the Special Collections Research Center, Temple University Libraries. Philadelphia, PA 19122)*

For decades, the Troop held casual Friday night horse shows in Valley Forge. Young ladies from the Radnor Pony Club would come, and Troopers would bring their daughters to ride. As William Rawle recalled, "Our wives would come along and we'd go over jumps, with someone acting as judge and sitting with a keg of beer next to the ring. We gave out ribbons and awards both for Troopers and for their wives or girlfriends."

Each year, the Troop continued (and continues today) to hold the Border Plate riding competition, where tensions could run quite high.

For example, a Troop captain once insisted on holding the Border Plate at Radnor Hunt because he fancied himself an expert on that particular course. His plot was foiled however, when another Trooper, Elkins Wetherill—a bitter rival at the Philadelphia Stock Exchange, and a much more accomplished horseman—entered the event to challenge him. The captain rode all out, determined to best his rival, but midway around the outside course, his horse took an abrupt turn near a tractor, tossing him into a wagon full of manure.

*Guests watch equitation at the 1964 Border Plate while Scholar Anwar Kemal rides toward them in the left foreground. (Photo from Anwar Kemal)*

For weeks before each Border Plate, Troopers on the Active Roll would form work parties to prepare the grounds, paint fences, cut grass, and order food. As Andrew Markle recalled, "There was a strict understanding that anyone who enjoyed spiffing up in a blazer and tie for evening cocktails at the Border Plate had to be equally comfortable sweating his ass off doing grounds work before the event. We never outsourced anything."

On competition day, contestants arrived early in the morning while spectators rolled in from as far afield as New York, Virginia, Maine, and Florida, many of them in classic or antique cars stored in barns all year in reserve for tailgating picnics. A panel judged the tailgates, giving an award to the best spread. In addition to riding events, the Border Plate would also feature side events such as hot air balloon rides and target shooting. Following the target shooting were cookouts, a barn dance, and finally a bonfire to keep festivities going through the night and into dawn.

*Border Plate picnic, 1964. (Photo by Anwar Kemal)*

*At the Border Plate, Troopers and guests (the ladies dressed in sundresses) pull out whatever firearms they have in their car trunks and shoot at targets while exercising military range disciplines. (Photo by Alix Cummin)*

*Trooper dismounts from horse while balancing his glass. (First City Troop Collection)*

# Chapter 16

# The Boyer Scholarship

On March 7, 1954, John Francis Boyer died in a car accident at age 23. Although this young Trooper's death was a terrible tragedy for his family, it transformed the First City Troop experience for many who followed him.

Raised in Chestnut Hill (a handsome Philadelphia neighborhood with strong Troop affiliations), Boyer had deployed with the Troop to Bavaria in 1952. While there, he was amazed at how well he got along with local Germans—the very people his father's generation had fought during both World Wars. He returned home fascinated with international affairs, convinced that future wars could be avoided if people from different nations had more opportunities to get to know each other on casual terms. He attended the 1953 Youth World Conference in Yugoslavia as an American delegate, but died before he could apply himself to his aims.

The tragedy of John Boyer's death was enhanced because he and his father Francis had only just recently become friends. The elder Boyer worked long hours as president and then CEO of Smith Kline & French Laboratories (now GlaxoSmithKline), which limited the time he spent at home while his son was growing up. A tie that united both men, however, was their love for the First City Troop. At the time of John Boyer's death, he and his father had just come to appreciate each other as military comrades.

In 1954, Francis honored his son by donating what would have been his inheritance to start the Boyer Scholarship Fund, an international scholarship dedicated to the romance of foreign exchange. Each year, a competition would be held to select both a Junior Trooper at home and a foreign recipient who could study any subjects they wanted. While the Trooper could travel abroad wherever he wished, the foreigner would come to Philadelphia to take his place. The foreigner would thus assume the American Trooper's identity within the unit, attending military training exercises in his stead.

*An American Boyer Scholar in Paris. Each year, the Trooper who wins this scholarship is encouraged to design his own program from scratch and to fend for himself while overseas. To that end, the scholarship's directors deliberately refrain from telling its recipients how to spend their time and money. When abroad, the young Trooper is encouraged to "go native," to absorb local customs like young Englishmen of old who completed their educations by traveling on the continental Grand Tour. (First City Troop collection)*

Often the Foreign Boyer would study at the University of Pennsylvania, which was easy enough to arrange since a Penn trustee always sat on the Boyer Scholarship's board of directors.

Francis Boyer hoped that foreign and domestic scholarship recipients would help the Troop form an extended family network internationally just as it always had among Philadelphians at home. By any reckoning, that aim was quickly achieved, and the scholarship continues to flavor—and almost dominate—the First Troop experience today.

When Charlie Davis won the scholarship in 1957, it changed his life. As he recalled, "They gave me $4,000 in 1957 to study in Italy, which back then was *real* money. Lunch was 25 cents, including a half bottle of wine. Before going to Italy, I'd never traveled anywhere, really. When I experienced life there, the scales fell from my eyes." Davis' daughter Alix explained, "Like many people from the Philadelphia area, Dad's insular upbringing centered on Cape May, the Main Line, and the Haverford School. Sure, he went to Penn, but it was Penn in his own back yard. When he went abroad, he was surprised to find he had a gift for understanding different cultures. Not in an academic way, but intuitively. Since that time, the friendships he made through the Boyer scholarship are some of the best friendships he's ever had."

The year Davis went to Italy as an American Boyer Scholar, Klaus Naude came to Philadelphia from Germany to take his place in the Troop. Naude grew up in depressed post-war Germany, son of a German General Staff officer who had competed in the Modern Pentathlon at the 1932 Los Angeles Olympics. (The family's Gallic name stemmed from Huguenot ancestors, who fled to Prussia generations earlier to escape French religious persecution.)

Klaus learned about the Boyer Scholarship through an indirect connection. Before the war, his parents were best friends with a Jewish couple, the Salmsons, who left Nazi Germany in the mid-1930s to settle in Philadelphia. Both families kept in touch over the ensuing decades. Mr. Salmson got a job in Philadelphia at Smith Kline French, where he worked for Francis Markoe "Koey" Rivinus, a First City Troop stalwart who helped found the Boyer Scholarship. After the war, the Salmsons returned to Germany to offer help to Naude's mother, whose husband had been killed on the Russian Front. Mr. Salmson took young Klaus aside, explained the Boyer Scholarship to him and urged him to apply. Klaus obeyed, applied, and won.

In Philadelphia, Klaus Naude studied at the Wharton School, served as a junior Trooper, and soon found himself nestled in the bosom of one of America's most insular urban gentries. Taking stock of his situation, he thought, "I seem to have landed in a good place!" With an American girlfriend on his arm and an extended family in the making through the First City Troop, he asked Captain Henry Glendenning if he could become an American citizen.

Chuckling years later, Naude said, "It was almost cute. While I was excited to become an American, my new friends seemed thrilled that I was choosing to live in Philadelphia. The city was so parochial back then! Locals were proud of the city's history. They worried that their young folk would to be lured to the excitement of New York, but they also gave an impression that Philadelphia was a *big deal* in its own right, when of course [he says with a hint of conspiracy] it really wasn't!" He chuckled after that last remark, with that fond familiar sort of smile—part love and part exasperated rolling of the eyes—that can only ever be reserved for Philadelphia.

Through hard work (and Troop connections), Naude landed a job at Fidelity Trust—whose Broad Street headquarters which would later be the setting for the fictional firm "Duke and Duke" in the cult classic film *Trading Places*. Each morning as he walked into Fidelity's lobby, Naude would glance up at a looming portrait of Gouverneur "Gouvey" Cadwalader, a locally respected banker, sportsman, decorated Marine Corps veteran, and First City Trooper. Naude felt that Cadwalder seemed to give provenance to the bank simply by his presence, and that his portrait was in the lobby was almost an advertisement, saying, *Gouvey Cadwalder Works Here*.

Naude's first impressions of the Philadelphia business scene are noteworthy because they occurred a decade before mergers and acquisitions would gut the city's locally owned firms in the 1970s and 80s. At the time of his arrival, there were quite a few Philadelphia companies whose executives and trustees had once served as privates in the First City Troop. In addition to Smith, Kline & French, and a number of quiet law firms, the Pennsylvania Railroad, Sunoco, First Pennsylvania Bank, Philadelphia Savings Fund Society (PSFS), Girard Trust, Provident National Bank, Fidelity Trust, Butcher & Singer, the Philadelphia Stock Exchange, Philadelphia Contributionship (America's first insurance company, founded by Benjamin Franklin), and the Insurance Company of North America (co-founded by a Trooper in 1792) all held strong Troop connections. Non-active and Honorary Troopers in these companies happily deferred business priorities to meet their Trooper-employee's Army requirements.

For example, Peter Clauss said, "One week, I had to leave the office for an Inspector General review at the Armory. My immediate boss and I were doing a labor intensive IPO at the time. He disliked the Troop and tried to keep me from attending the IG inspection at the Armory. But his boss, who was a Trooper, said, 'Let him go! The IG inspection is more important!'"

The Boyer Scholarship has influenced so many people, both foreign and domestic, that it has taken on a life of its own beyond the First City Troop. For example, it may have helped thaw United States-China relations in the late 1960s.

This occurred when Boyer Scholar Anwar Kemal returned home to join the Foreign Service in his native Pakistan after spending two years with the Troop in 1964-65. On a diplomatic train ride from Bejing to Shanghi, young Kemal found himself in deep conversation with Zou Enlai, Mao Zedong's Premier, who peppered Kemal with questions about his recent experiences in Philadelphia. Kemal described America in glowing terms, and insisted that the Chinese would benefit greatly from renewed diplomatic ties with the United States. Within less than a year, Henry Kissinger made his secret trip to China, followed by President Nixon's publicized trip in 1972.

*Charlie Davis, Klaus Naude, Anwar Kemal and other grateful Boyer Scholar recipients celebrate the program at a reunion in 2015. According to Honorary Troop Captain Charlie Meredith, "Anwar Kemal's cameo role in helping to thaw relations between Red China and the U.S. is the perfect example of the Boyer Scholarship's mission. John Boyer believed that the world could become safer with college age students traveling and interacting with other nations' young students." (Photo by Ryan Noyes)*

## Chapter 17

# Honorary Trooper Biddle

There are three types of Troop membership—Active, Non-active, and Honorary. Active Troopers are those currently serving in the National Guard. Non-actives are those who have finished their military enlistments, but who remain in the Troop for ever after as fraternal members. The Honorary Roll is reserved for those with twenty years in service, or for special "guest stars" who get elected later in life on the basis of other special merits. General John J. Pershing joined the Troop in this manner, as did President Dwight David Eisenhower.

In 1960, Anthony J. Drexel Biddle was elected to the Honorary Roll—a man who couldn't have been better suited the Troop's best imaginary image of itself. Biddle's impressive and somewhat quirky career outlines in caricature a number of traits that have characterized various Gentlemen of Gloucester since 1774.

Born into Philadelphia's most well-respected family, Biddle left boarding school at the outbreak of World War I to enlist in the army as the only white private in an otherwise all-black African American unit. After seeing combat, he returned home a major. Two decades later, as a United States ambassador to Poland, he befriended fellow diplomat Joe Kennedy's son John, and took him under his wing for a time in Warsaw in 1939. That visit was cut short however, when the Germans invaded in 1939.

*As Stukas fly overhead, the raw-boned Biddle loads State Department documents into his car trunk to evacuating the United States embassy in Warsaw. (This photo appeared in various news sources in October, 1939)*

In wartime London, as United States emissary to governments-in-exile of Belgium, Czechoslovakia, Greece, Luxembourg, the Netherlands, Norway, and Yugoslavia, Biddle met an assertive Frenchman called de Gaulle, who claimed to be the true leader of Free France, who had difficulty making friends. As one of the few people to take de Gaulle seriously, Biddle won the future leader's trust for the rest of his life.

Biddle's son, Tony, explained that although his father was friendly with President Franklin D. Roosevelt, he was "sickened" with FDR's promises to Stalin at the Yalta Conference, which negated many of the promises Biddle had personally made to European heads of state during the war. To protect his conscience, Biddle resigned from the State Department in 1944 and joined the Army as lieutenant colonel. He served on General Eisenhower's staff, where his contacts

117

with underground movements in occupied nations helped provide intelligence for planning Operation Overlord, the allied invasion of Europe. He continued on Eisenhower's staff, supervising European reconstruction after the war ended.

Eisenhower was so impressed with Biddle's capacity as an all-rounder that he asked him to be his presidential running mate. Biddle declined, stating that a) he preferred to operate behind the scenes and b) he was Democrat. Although Biddle may have preferred to keep out of the limelight, he had been a much-photographed "fashion plate" since youth, who would later be named the "best dressed man in America" in a still-famous *Esquire Magazine* article titled "The Art of Wearing Clothes."

Disappointed that Biddle wouldn't run for office with him (Biddle also turned down a request to run for Governor of Pennsylvania), Ike asked if there were any other posts he might want. Biddle replied that he would take anything that would allow him to live in Pennsylvania. Eisenhower jumped on the offer, telling Biddle that the Pennsylvania National Guard was giving him political problems at the time. Biddle resigned from the Army and became Adjutant General of the PA Guard.

According to his son, of all the posts Biddle ever held, he was proudest of being Pennsylvania Adjutant General. Through much effort, he solved the political problems that Eisenhower had assigned to him, while living in a farm house at Fort Indiantown Gap that he remodeled to suit his tastes. During that period, Biddle often entertained visiting members of the First City Troop who were family friends.

In those years, Biddle's son often answered the phone to hear a gruff French-sounding voice crackling long distance on the other end of the line. It was de Gaulle, who would call a few times each week, claiming that Biddle was the only American he really trusted. In addition to calls from de Gaulle, Biddle also heard quite a bit from John F. Kennedy, his young buddy from Warsaw, who now turned to him for moral support whenever he hit low points in his career. Whenever JFK said he wanted to leave politics, Biddle encouraged him to keep at it.

When Kennedy succeeded Eisenhower in the White House, a crisis flared up in Spain about the island of Gibraltar. Kennedy asked Biddle to go to Spain, explaining that he needed someone "simpatico" enough to deal with the Spanish— someone who could combine military bearing with diplomatic warmth. Though very reluctant to leave Pennsylvania, Biddle went to Spain for a while and managed to accomplish what the President asked him to do.

Biddle remained in touch with the First City Troopers during all this time, and because he exemplified so many characteristics that Troopers held dear, he was elected to the Honorary Roll. Sadly, Biddle didn't live much longer after he became a Trooper. Although physically fit, performing hundreds of pushups daily, his three-pack-a-day cigarette smoking habit ultimately got the better of him. He died in 1961 at age 63.

When considering Biddle's life, a series of seemingly contradictory character traits appear that have appeared frequently among First City Troopers over the years—such as 1) the way he enlisted as a private in World War I, even though he could have been an officer; 2) the way he was equally

119

comfortable with hard military service and "simpatico" diplomacy; 3) the way he left or turned down a series of high-ranking posts that more career-oriented men would have seized with a vise-like grip; 4) the way he refused to be Eisenhower's presidential running mate but embraced the (much) more parochial role as Adjutant General in the Pennsylvania Guard; and 4) the way he combined diligence about physical fitness training with laxity about excessive cigarette smoking.

This somewhat confusing—but certainly charming—jumble of traits reflects a value system that has characterized First City Troopers since 1774 and which remains part of the unit's cultural inheritance today.

*Adjutant General Biddle reviews the 28th Infantry Division in this undated photo at Fort Indiantown Gap. (First City Troop collection)*

# Chapter 18

# The Vietnam Era

In 1963, the National Guard gave the Troop a new official unit designation—Troop A, 1st Squadron/ 223rd Cavalry—while also allowing it to retain its full traditional name—First Troop Philadelphia City Cavalry (FTPCC). To the disappointment of many Troopers, their unit now reported to the squadron commander (a lieutenant colonel) instead of to the division commander (a major general), which added layers of unwelcome bureaucracy between First City and high command. Along with this change, the Troop was also forced to increase its manpower yet again, necessitating the recruitment of more men. The Cold War draft made recruiting easy, of course, but many of the older members feared that size increases would yield a corresponding dilution of quality.

As college undergraduates flooded the Active Roll, they drove down Troop's median age until there were few enlisted men over 23 years old and few officers over 32. Although such an age range was common in regular cavalry units, it was uncommon for the Troop. Youth brought rambunctiousness and a rise in discipline problems that reflected not only the age of the newest Troopers, but also the spirit of the 1960s. As a result, the 1960s and 70s would become a chapter in Troop history that later generation would call (with feelings both of admiration and head-shaking) "the wild years." Amusing anecdotes from the 1960s and 70s abound in Troop lore.

*Troopers relax in the back of an M-113 armored personnel carrier at annual training in 1964. (Photo by Anwar Kemal)*

For example, on a hot and muggy summer morning in 1966, wide-eyed and newly enlisted Private First Class James Blunt picked up the orderly room telephone and only faintly heard a voice crackling on the other end of what seemed to be a long-distance line. It was Corporal Claud Beer (whom Blunt had never met before) calling from London. Yes, Beer understood that the Troop had just assembled at the Armory, and that they were just about to convoy down to Camp Pickett, Virginia for annual training, but would Private Blunt please tell Platoon Sergeant Winslow Lewis that Beer wouldn't be in this morning, and would be sure to catch up with the Troop in a few days? You see, Beer was at a high-stakes backgammon tournament in Mayfair, and it "wasn't convenient" for him to get away from the table at the moment. Eager to please, the fresh-faced Blunt obediently relayed this message to Lewis, only to absorb a vitriolic broadside as the hapless messenger.

122

According to Blunt, three days later, "just as the Troop was standing in formation for roll call after lunch, the entire company looked on archly as a gleaming black Rolls-Royce ghosted into view and purred to a stop on the dusty company street. A liveried chauffeur hopped out smartly, first fetching Claude's duffel bag and portable backgammon board from the boot, and then opening the rear door for his young charge." It was Claud Beer, just in from London. As a hundred men snorted and doubled over, writhing to contain their laughter, Platoon Sergeant Lewis stood seething and most unamused. Lewis pounced on Beer like a lion, assigning him to perpetual kitchen and guard duty for the next two weeks. Fascinated by this mysterious Trooper who made his living as a professional backgammon player, Blunt tagged along with Beer on his endless guard rounds through the motor pool. Blunt recalled, "Any of the finer points about backgammon that I might have learned from Beer that week were lost on me, overshadowed as they were by his thrilling descriptions of Mayfair night life."

*(Previous page) Troopers lumber into formation in the 1960s on a day not unlike the day when Claude Beer made his much noticed arrival by Rolls Royce. (Photo by Anwar Kemal)*

As the Vietnam War escalated in the late 1960s, draft-age men across the United States flocked to National Guard units to avoid deploying to Southeast Asia. Quite a few joined the First City Troop for this very reason, many of them commuting from New York City and Washington D.C., converging on Philadelphia by rail on drill weekends. But not everyone in the Troop wanted to avoid Vietnam.

When Charlie McIlvaine joined the Troop in 1965 fresh from Chestnut Hill Academy, he had "every intention of going to Vietnam!" While tinkering with a powerful radio transmitter at the Armory one drill weekend, McIlvaine picked up radio traffic from a live firefight in Vietnam. Thrilled to hear the chatter of men communicating in actual combat, he and fellow Junior Trooper Newton DeRiemer decided to petition Secretary of Defense Robert McNamara to send their unit to Vietnam. For months they sent letters pestering McNamara, but of course, they never received a response.

*(Previous page, this page, and next page) Snapshots of Troopers, friends, and family in the 1960s show young people who didn't seem much influenced by hippie counterculture, free love, and Woodstock. In Philadelphia, large segments of society still looked back to the 1950s when behavior was based on much older patterns—when men weren't fully dressed without neckties. (Photos by Anwar Kemal)*

In 1967 and 1968, Captain Jerry Cummin received notice that the Troop might deploy to Vietnam. He responded to this warning order by doubling the Troop's drill schedule to two weekends per month, and training the men more rigorously than he had before. After a year of intense preparation, the Troop was abruptly ordered to stand down. Twenty years later, Cummin discovered that just as the Troop was about to be sent to Vietnam, the Texas governor interceded and asked for a unit from his state to go instead. Military reports from that time reveal that had the Troop been deployed, it would have been ready for service. After a combat fitness test in 1967, a regular Army evaluator wrote, "In 22 years of active duty, I have never seen a better trained troop-size unit, including the active Army, National Guard, and reserves. I would be willing to enter combat with your troop tomorrow."

The Troop spent much of its training time in the 1960s rehearsing riot control scenarios in preparation for anti-war demonstrations that broke out on college campuses across the country. Although mob control had been one of the Troop's principal roles since the 1770s, this time around, they carved an amusing niche on the other side of the equation (on drill weekends at least), by *staging* riots rather than quelling them.

As Charlie McIlvaine explained, "We became the de-facto riot-training unit [for National Guard units] throughout the state. They would have us act as rioters, so other units could practice putting us down. Each day, we'd eat breakfast, and then go outside to be rioters, which ended with everyone getting tear-gassed. Then we'd eat a nice lunch, and go outside to be rioters all over again. Some guys were tear-gassed so often that they built up immunity to the effects of the gas. So, before the gas cleared, they'd take off their masks and pretend the air had cleared, luring the other side to take theirs off. The other guys would breathe in the tear gas and start gagging, and we would roar with laughter." As the unit's official history dryly recorded, "the entire Troop was cast as the ruthless mob, with predictable results."

In the mid-1950s an English Boyer Scholar introduced rugby to the Troop, and it quickly replaced polo as the unit's favorite team sport. George Connell embraced the game with such enthusiasm that he played for the next forty years, leaving the field reluctantly at age 69.

For a few decades, the National Guard allowed rugby tournaments to count as military physical training, which allowed the Troop to field a nationally ranked team, battling local prep schools, Yale, Penn, and Princeton. In 1968, they even made it to national championships, where faced New York's formidable Old Blue Rugby Football Club. By the end of that match, both teams were tied at zero, and George Connell found himself in the scrum five yards from the New York's goal line despairing that Old Blue "Goliath" would beat First City Troop "David." Then suddenly, the entire New York line stood up, allowing a surprised Connell to scramble through them and score! Astonished at this sudden victory, the flabbergasted Connell wondered what on earth could have caused Old Blue to do such a self-defeating thing. The answer to this question brings him to tears of laughter even today. It turns out that Teddy Gilbert (the same man who illegally helped the Germans launch their first post-World-War-Two airplane) who was also in that scrum, caused Old Blue to "freak out" by leaning forward and kissing his opposite square in the face.

*First City Troop Rugby Team, wearing brown, buff, and gold colors inherited from the Gloucester Hunt Club. The Troop once fielded so many rugby players that it had A, B, and C teams. (The "C" stood for Cocktails.) When the National Guard stopped allowing rugby to count as military fitness training in the mid-1970s, the First City Troop Rugby Team disbanded. It was later resurrected as the Second City Troop Rugby Club, a stand-alone entity. (Photo from Mike Codell)*

While the Troop never went to Vietnam as a unit, some of its members deployed individually, serving in the CIA, Special Forces, and flying secret missions for Air America.

Tony Abbott and Nick Sellers left the Troop's Active Roll to join the Army Special Forces (Green Berets). Both of them stand out as quintessential "Gentlemen of Gloucester." A rich Trooper who grew up in a handsome Main Line house bedecked with Rembrandt Peale paintings (Peale was an ancestor), Sellers was a lawyer by profession, who would attend annual training with fourteen uniforms pressed and starched so he could wear a fresh one each day. He took his National Guard duties very seriously.

Abbott was younger than Sellers. He joined the Troop while still at Chestnut Hill Academy and remained in the unit while studying at Princeton University. As the junior-most Trooper, Abbott was assigned to Sellers's platoon, where Sellers provided "guidance and assurance that gave [Abbott] confidence to deal with all those older and hardened Troopers." The older Troopers opened doors to a world of action and adventure that fascinated the young Abbott. He learned about scuba diving from Dick Walling, and then went to Florida to become a commercial diver and charter boat captain. Enjoying the physically active lifestyle, Abbott soon re-joined the military to attend Infantry OCS, Airborne, Ranger, Pathfinder, Special Forces, and Vietnamese language schools.

Unbeknownst to Abbott, around that same time, Sellers also re-enlisted and went through the same training regimen. Already proficient in French, Sellers skipped language training and went straight to Vietnam (where French was commonly spoken), to the Special Forces camp on Phu Quoc Island, off the southern coast of Vietnam near Cambodia. Soon after Sellers settled into his new duties, a routine helicopter touched down on Phu Quoc, and off stepped the fresh-faced Abbott.

Abbott and Sellers participated in a number Special Forces activities, such as working in training camps, running counter guerrilla operations, performing cross-border raids into North Vietnam, Laos, and Cambodia, watching the Ho Chi Minh Trail, recovering downed pilots, and setting ambushes. During these operations, Abbott received two minor wounds in firefights, and Sellers received a severe leg wound. While recovering at a hospital in Saigon, Sellers was forbidden to return to his unit until he could walk without crutches. Anxious to get back to the field, but still unable to walk unaided, he fashioned a brace for his leg beneath his loose fatigues and grimaced as he limped out of the hospital.

While commanding a Special Forces detachment and a battalion of CIDG (Civil Irregular Defense Group) at Ha Tien on the Mekong Delta, Sellers found time to write *The Princes of Ha Tien*, a book describing the unique politics of the Ha Tien region near Cambodia, which had once been ruled by philosopher-princes.

After Vietnam, Sellers returned to his Philadelphia law practice and later became an educator and judge. Like many First City Troopers, he developed a life-long taste for military service. He re-entered the Pennsylvania National Guard and eventually retired as a brigadier general. Abbott went on to command the Underwater Swimmers and ParaScuba/Rescue School, which served as the Apollo Recovery Team for Central and South America. He would later say, "The Troop prepared me for leadership in the Special Forces because both organizations don't give a damn about a man's title or rank. The only thing that matters is each person's talents and abilities relative to the task at hand." Abbott eventually refused a promotion to the rank of major because he didn't want to be "trapped behind a desk."

While working with the Apollo Recovery Program, Abbott nearly crossed paths with another Trooper—Pete Conrad—a famous astronaut.

*Nick Sellers (above) and Tony Abbott (below). (Photos from Tony Abbott)*

Conrad grew up in the Philadelphia area, living in the carriage house of what had been his parents' estate before the Stock Market crash of 1929. A bright boy who struggled with dyslexia, he thrived in the First City Troop. After discovering a love for aviation while working as a teen at Paoli Airfield, he learned to fly, and then left the Active Roll to become a naval aviator. As a crack pilot, he entered NASA's astronaut selection process and eventually commanded the Apollo 12 lunar mission. In 1969, Conrad became the third astronaut (and first Trooper) to walk on the moon.

*Pete Conrad, the first Trooper on the Moon. Before embarking on his lunar mission, an Italian journalist challenged him by claiming that Neil Armstrong's "One small step for man" speech had not been his own words. To prove that NASA didn't script comments for astronauts, when Conrad stepped on the moon he yelled, "Whoopee! Man, that may have been a small one for Neil, but that's a long one for me." (First City Troop collection)*

# Chapter 19

# After the Gates Commission

Through a curious historical twist, the Cold War draft that helped the Troop fill its ranks came to an end through the efforts of an Honorary Trooper—Thomas Sovereign Gates, Jr.—who, as head of President Richard Nixon's Gates Commission, recommended that Nixon end the draft in 1970. Nixon demurred for a while but finally stopped the draft in 1973.

Like numerous Gentlemen of Gloucester before him, Gates brought flair to the American Establishment in ways that amused people around him. JP Morgan historian Ron Chernow described him as a rich, affable "cowboy in well-tailored suits [aka First City Trooper]" who "gave off an easy air of authority, an engaging conviviality. A macho hero to subordinates, he loved wine, women, and warplanes." After serving as an enlisted Trooper in the 1930s, he became a Naval Air Intelligence Commander in the Pacific and Mediterranean theatres during World War II. As President Dwight Eisenhower's Secretary of the Navy and Secretary of Defense, he authorized U-2 spy plane missions (including the one in which Francis Gary Powers was shot down over Russia) and helped define the nation's nuclear and strategic-weapons policy. After working for Eisenhower, Gates joined Morgan Guaranty Trust Company, becoming president, CEO, and chairman in the 1960s. In 1985, the United States Navy named a Ticonderoga-class cruiser after him.

Today, Gates's photo hangs on the wall behind the bar at the Troop's NCO Club. Identified by name and Troop number only—with no indication of his rank or life accomplishments—he appears wearing the same dress uniform as a young man in the 1920s that his modern counterparts wear today. Although he held many important posts during his career, his main importance from the Troop's standpoint is that he served as an enlisted man in the unit just like everyone else.

*President and Mrs. Nixon visit the Armory. (Troop History: 1948-1991)*

When the draft ended, National Guard enrollments across the country dropped precipitously. The Troop's membership plunged from 154 to 110 men in one year, causing the 28th Infantry Division to threaten the unit's existence. Responsibility now fell to the so-called "draft-dodgers" to keep the Troop alive. Although many of them fled the Guard as soon as they could, enough decided to stay on the Active Roll to raise manpower back to a sufficient level.

*Many men who joined the Troop during the Vietnam draft remained with the unit for decades longer than they originally expected and helped retain the unit's esprit de corps. (Photo from James Blunt)*

After Vietnam, a new breed of enlistee emerged: prior-service military officers who resigned their commissions in other branches to join First City as privates and NCOs. For example, John Warlow, an Army engineer officer with an interest in riding, resigned his commission to join the Troop as an enlisted man. Alexander Kerr, a Reserve Officer Training Corps (ROTC) graduate of Yale University, joined up after learning about the unit from friends at his Philadelphia law firm. He served as an NCO for a while, eventually resumed his commission, and then became Troop Captain.

Roy West attended his first Troop dinner in 1970 while working in the advertising industry and serving as a Naval Reserve officer. He initially wrote the organization off as "a bunch of rich draft dodgers," but was fascinated by the cavalier culture at the Armory. When he sat down to eat that night, he thought, "What the hell have I walked into?" Compared with the restrained manner of United States Navy wardrooms, the Troop was wild. He said, "Then I *realized*. This was a *cavalry* mess! Cavalry units the world over have always had a reputation for rambunctiousness. These guys did everything but jump horses over the tables!"

West returned to join the Troop ten years later. By that time, half the Active Roll had logged prior-service tours in the regular Army, Navy, Air Force, and Marine Corps. He felt that Marines fit most easily into the Troop: "You'll be surprised to hear this, but the Marine Corps has historically been an adjunct of the Philadelphia Social Register. The Main Line always sent its bookish sons into the Navy and it's jocks into the Marines. Franklin Wharton, William Phillip Biddle, Smedley Butler, and Anthony Drexel Biddle Sr. were all Philadelphians who helped define Marine Corps culture over the years."

An inter-service mix was nothing new for the Troop, of course. For two centuries, its members had often left the unit for leadership roles in other service branches. But now the process was moving in reverse: former officers were finishing their careers in the Troop instead of joining the unit as younger men in order to start them. As each man brought the culture of his prior service branch with him, he helped cross-pollinate the Troop's institutional gene pool.

*2010 Harvard Business Review explored cultural strengths and weaknesses based on trade-offs each branch of military service makes between "process" and "flexibility." The Troop greatly benefited from blending the perspectives of former Army, Navy, Air Force, and Marine Corps officers. (Photo from A. T. W. Lamacowitz)*

A 2010 Harvard Business Review article, *Which of These People is your Future NCO?* explored this dynamic from a corporate leadership perspective, explaining how veterans tend to demonstrate strengths and weaknesses based on the military branch in which they served. Each service branch makes a trade-off between *process* and *flexibility*, favoring one over the other. "The Navy and Air Force engender a process orientation; the Army and Marines emphasize flexibility.

137

Former Army and Marine Corps officers depend less on familiarity with the firms as they transition to leadership roles. Former Navy and Air Force officers perform well in highly regulated industries. Executives with Army and Marine Corps experience do better in small companies than in large ones. Executives with Navy and Air Force experience excel in firms with a process approach to innovation."

As the First City Troop gained former officers from all branches, it was increasingly able to draw on a broad spectrum of approaches. Marines brought their wry sense of humor, aversion to complaining, and bias for directness and simplicity. Airmen and sailors brought managerial, procedural, and bureaucratic skills, which counterbalanced the Troop's cavalier penchant for flamboyance and dilettantism. Special Forces men leavened the lump with their own strain of outside-the-box thinking.

In addition to recruiting prior-service officers, the Troop made efforts to recruit younger men fresh from home. Karl Schoettle lavished special attention on revamping the election process to help attract boys from prep schools and colleges. He believed the Troop had special things to teach them about leadership that they could not find elsewhere, declaring, "I knew quite a few Troopers who said they learned more about leadership from two weeks at NCO School than they got from a year at Wharton." He explored every angle to determine how Troop membership could most benefit young people. Among these, he identified leadership development, business networking, patriotism, camaraderie, and love of history as the chief factors. To his surprise, when speaking with students, he found their greatest motivation for joining the Troop was "love of history."

Fighting the strong anti-military bias that swept through schools and colleges in the wake of Vietnam, Schoettle visited the local prep schools and colleges that had historically provided the Troop with its members. Many of these schools, such as Episcopal Academy, Haverford School, Chestnut Hill Academy, Germantown Academy, and Penn Charter, still had alumni on the Non-active and Honorary Rolls. The Troop's traditionally favored boarding schools, such as the Hill School, Lawrenceville, St. Paul's (New Hampshire) and St. George's (Rhode Island) figured less into the new equation for logistical reasons. Princeton, University of Pennsylvania, and small liberal arts colleges like Trinity, Washington & Lee, and Hampden-Sydney remained feeders, as did West Point, Virginia Military Institute, and Citadel.

Schoettle hosted faculty members from some of these schools at Armory cocktail parties, but he would also resort to spectacular stunts, such as driving tanks and armored vehicles to a campus, or arriving on horseback. He chuckled, "Pious anti-military faculty members were outraged at us for showing up like this, but the kids loved it!"

*(Above and below) When the Draft ended in 1973, the Troop had to actively recruit new members for the first time since World War II. (Troop History: 1948-1991)*

# Chapter 20

# Fun and Games

In order to retain their 18th century tradition of voluntary service, Troopers donated their National Guard drill pay each month to the unit's treasurer without ever seeing a cent. John Gallagher, the Troop's full-time Readiness NCO, was the only man in the unit to draw a salary. A natural fixer and wizard at navigating the Army's bureaucratic maze, he not only received normal military pay, he got a *stipend* (and the Troop paid for his sons to go to the Haverford School).

This occurred because, throughout his career, the Army would periodically re-assign his Readiness NCO job to lower and lower ranks. The Troop valued him so much in this role that they asked him to accept whatever rank reductions were necessary to keep the position. In return, they made up his original salary difference with their own money.

Gallagher had a keen sense of historical humor. For example, when new Troopers had to get physical exams, he would sometimes fill out their medical forms as if he were the doctor, signing as "Dr. Benjamin Rush." As every Trooper knew, Rush was the 18th century father of Philadelphia medicine, a renaissance man, signer of the Declaration of Independence, member of Continental Congress, Surgeon General of the Continental Army, and founder of Dickinson College. However, it never occurred to clerks at the 28th

Division headquarters in Harrisburg that "Dr. Rush" had been in a Philadelphia cemetery since 1813—*why would it?*

When Gallagher finally retired from the Army, his successor attempted to carry on the impersonation. But on his first attempt to send a batch of Benjamin Rush signatures to Harrisburg, an eagle-eyed clerk instantly saw the discrepancy. The clerk called the Armory and said "Now listen here, we have records of medical forms signed by Dr. Benjamin Rush going back twenty years. The signature you sent us doesn't match that one. It's an obvious forgery!"

*Thanks to Readiness NCO John Gallagher, a number of Troopers competed in elite sports while fulfilling their regular military duties. Charles Horter (above left) won a bronze medal in Dragon class sailing at the 1972 Munich Olympics. (Photo from Charles Horter)*

Speaking of forgeries, Tony Morris (a direct descendant Samuel Morris) recalled a Trooper who donated his riding mower for the men to use on lawn detail at Fort Indiantown

Gap. But with eccentric thoroughness, he didn't just bring a civilian lawn mower to drill and leave it at that. Instead, he painted it olive drab, stenciled military decals, and drew up official-seeming documents to make a paper trail for the "vehicle." One day a visiting officer inspecting the unit spotted the suspicious looking lawnmower and demanded to see documentation for it. Cool as can be, the Trooper handed him an oil-stained, olive drab canvas army-issue document case containing the typical logbook used for all military vehicles. The logbook inside meticulously showed mileage, fuel and oil fillings and a complete service record dating back months and months. After flipping through the paper work, the officer tossed it back at the Trooper's chest, sternly carried on with the rest of his inspection, and then doubled up laughing when he walked around the corner away from view.

One reason so many Troopers remained on the Active Roll after the draft ended was that nothing in civilian life could match the amount of fun to be had with the lads on drill weekends. After all, camaraderie is what motivates people to spend decades in National Guard units (and volunteer fire companies) across the country.

Now as every soldier knows, 90% of the time spent on duty involves standing around with nothing much to do. In the 1970s, Troopers solved this problem by playing backgammon—loads of it. Indeed, they went wild for the game.

Platoon sergeants included backgammon sets on their official equipment lists. During home drill weekends, they ran tournaments inside vehicles and in every room at the Armory—even in empty shower stalls. If a sergeant saw a group of privates standing idle, he would *command* them to play backgammon. Senior NCOs kept score for unit-wide competitions on a big board in the TOC (Tactical Operations Center), with participants' names disguised to look like a roster of field vehicle placements. The backgammon tradition continued for decades afterward. When I joined the unit in 2004, a Trooper from New York City would arrive on drill weekends in his Lotus Elise with a second wallet tucked into his breast pocket dedicated exclusively for backgammon betting.

In addition to backgammon, Troopers one-upped each other with endless pranks and practical jokes. For example, while everyone was standing in formation on the first morning of summer camp one year, a recovery crane (discreetly hidden in an adjacent gully the night before) suddenly switched on and slowly swung its boom out over the soldiers lined up below. To their astonishment, a man dangled from the crane, attached by a shoulder harness of pistol belts, and rigidly assuming the position of attention. It was none other than First Sergeant Teddy Gilbert—the same man who helped the Germans launch their first post-war airplane and who kissed the Troop rugby team to victory against Old Blue! As he was perfectly lowered down into his normal place at in front of formation, the men erupted into double laughter when they realized that their First Sergeant was also *naked*.

Such stunts bred copycats for years afterward. Like that time when Trooper Dan Ott swung into first formation like Tarzan on a rope he tied to the Armory ceiling rafters the night before. In order to make the prank optimally effective, he had prearranged all the trucks in drill hall so that when he swung down the next morning, the entire Troop would be standing in position for him to land directly in the spot where he normally stood in his platoon.

In addition to dreaming up stunts, it was common for Troopers to wear field uniforms of their own invention. At annual training one year Ned Greene's sartorial choice for the summer heat was a quasi-military getup of cut-off camouflage shorts, Gucci loafers with bare feet, olive green Lacoste polo shirt from his mom, and a worn-out Vietnam boonie hat. A visiting general swept into the TOC (Tactical Operations Center) while Greene was wearing this outrageous costume while manning the radio. Greene sprang to his feet, snapped a salute, and braced himself for the broadside that was sure to follow. Overlooking the rest of Greene's rig, the general glared at his boonie hat and said, "Isn't your hat kind of frayed Private?" Without thinking, Greene shot back, "Sir, this hat aint afraid of *nobody*!" The general burst into laughter and Greene won the Troop's *Snappiest Answer to the Stupidest Question* award that year.

*(Previous page and below) The Troop's mess section was legendary. (Undated photos from Anwar Kemal and Troop collection)*

The Mess Section was a legendary. With their historical ties to the Schuylkill Fishing Company (an angling club more preoccupied with cooking and eating fish than catching them), Troopers ranked epicureanism a close third behind soldiering and horse riding. Food was such an important part of the culture, that when a Wall Street Journal reporter spent time with Troop in 1980, he summed up his experience with the following headline: "At Ease, Troopers: Fall Out for Caviar and Pickled Herring—That's the Order Often Heard at Elite Philadelphia Club, A Unit of the National Guard."

What made the mess section so charming was the inventive way they worked within the parameters of army-issue food to improve it by adding little magic touches. They tinkered with spices, combinations, and special sauces. The cooks might rise at 4 a.m. to bake fresh bread. They might whip up such niceties as Lobster Newberg over omelets, hearts-de-palm salad, "oysters on the halfs," or the headline-producing caviar and herring. They bargained with local farmers to swap military rations for freshly butchered steaks or smoked hams. For years, they performed these feats in a custom-designed field kitchen built into a normal-seeming deuce-and-a-half truck nicknamed the "War Wagon," which boasted three field stoves configured like galley stoves on a yacht. For special occasions, they even brought the Troop's silver service into the field.

For years, the mess section was orchestrated by the theatrical and mercurial John "Sammy" Means. A part-time actor and occasional print model, Means was physically striking and square-jawed, standing a clean 6'3" tall, with a commanding shock of white hair. He appeared as a maître d'hotel in the soap opera *All My Children* and had a visible (but non-speaking) role in the movie *Ghost Busters*. His real forte was to pose as the "CEO" in trade magazine and Wall Street Journal print advertisements. Whenever such a photo shoot required him to wear a jacket and tie, he would dutifully sport his Troop rosette. (Rosettes are described in detail in a chapter below.)

*John "Sammy" Means. (Bell Telephone advertisement, from John Warlow's collection)*

Means would bring four duffle bags and fourteen hard-starched fatigue uniforms to annual training each year, with each uniform on its own hanger, covered in plastic. One of these duffle bags would contain his personal effects, one his cooking provisions and the other *two* would be stuffed to capacity with plastic vodka bottles for himself and his cooks. He would normally consume one full bottle per day. Each morning, he would emerge from his tent wearing a fresh uniform (starched so stiffly that it made cracking sounds as he walked) and perfectly shined boots, with his jutting chin clean-shaven. Starting out looking thus letter perfect, he would begin working through the day's vodka handle. As each hour progressed, his appearance would unravel by degrees as he slowly drifted into slurred but still functioning inebriation. Regardless of his alcoholic intake however, his attention to mess duties rarely went slack—if anything, his dedication

148

inflamed. In his passion for culinary provision, he would subject senior officers to tongue lashings whenever he felt they were neglecting to feed their men properly in the field.

Alas, the noble mess section met its demise in the late 1980s when the 28th Infantry Division consolidated all company messes into one central hub at the battalion level. But mess or no mess, it was impossible to fully stamp out a 200-year commitment to good eating. Talents once devoted to the War Wagon now shifted to Ice Detail. Under this new arrangement, a group of Non-active Troopers would show up at drill weekends and annual training each year, to drive around in a mysterious vehicle, providing drinks and heavy hors d'oeuvres to all the men in the field.

Of course, like most "new ideas" in the Troop, the ice detail concept was actually recycled from something which had occurred in the past. We first hear mention of it in 1960, when a Trooper called Oliver Karrington Conver joined the Troop with a number of his Hill School cronies. At annual training that year, the Troop put him in command of a Hertz van rented to deliver food, ice, and drinks to the men in the field. Although the van's coloring was inauspicious for military use—it was brand new, bright red, and it stood out for miles—the men quickly remedied this by smearing the whole thing from tires to top with thick layers of mud.

Before the extended field exercise that week, Captain Henry Ingersoll ordered every man in the Troop to leave his wristwatch and wallet with Oliver in the van, reasoning that in a real war you wouldn't be carrying those things into combat. In addition to that, they dumped extra weapons into the van beyond what they needed for the exercise. Thus laden, Oliver now found himself navigating unfamiliar Camp Pickett,

Virginia in a brand new, absurdly mud-caked van, carrying forty to fifty expensive watches and wallets in the front cab, in addition to crates of booze and United States Army weapons in the back. Things went along well enough for a while—until he attempted to drive through the main gate.

The gate guards, bored from standing around all day swatting at mosquitoes and flies, came suddenly alert when Oliver's mysterious looking van squeaked to a halt in front of them. They started questioning him casually enough at first and then phoned for the MPs to come take a closer look. Oliver's initial nervousness morphed into stark terror when they began searching the whole vehicle. Astonished by the van's contents, and thrilled with the chance to arrest a real felon (and a Yankee to boot!), the MPs tossed luckless Oliver into jail and confiscated his truck. In a moment, the Troop lost one man, some weapons, and *all* its watches and wallets.

Things looked dire. Captain Ingersoll called Honorary Captain Stokes, who by that time was the squadron commander. At a loss, Stokes sent the following mayday to the Pennsylvania Adjutant General in Harrisburg: "The Ice Truck has been compromised!" Say no more," barked the general, "I'll handle this. You don't fuck with the Truck!" No one seems to know how the situation was worked out between the Commonwealths of Virginia and Pennsylvania, but Oliver, the van, and all its contents were released from captivity and allowed to cross the Mason-Dixon Line homeward.

By the late 1980s, the Troop's approach to Ice Trucks was much more thoroughly planned out. They bought a Ford van, painted it olive drab with genuine army paint, and printed fake (but realistic) designations on the side with actual army stencils. As Roy West recalls, "That was our Stealth Wagon.

The drivers followed us into the field to make certain that none of us lacked for anything, nor drew a sober breath."

By this point in its history, the Troop's drinking culture had become something of a game that inspired much creativity. Drinking was seen not just in terms of consumption but also as a cat-and-mouse game played out between the men and the commanding officers. Readers should recall that until the Navy's famous Tailhook scandal in the 1990s, alcohol consumption was a much larger part of military culture throughout the United States than it is today.

The best example of creative drinks mixing was certainly exhibited by Dixon Byecroft, IV, a talented mechanic and gentleman farmer whose source of income was never quite ascertained. He converted a World War II flamethrower into a gin-and-tonic dispenser that actually worked. At drill weekends and at annual training, he would carry it into the field during combat exercises, where he functioned incognito as a one-man ice detail. When regular Army inspectors asked why the Troop still had such an antiquated piece of equipment on its roster, Byecroft claimed it was left over from the Korean War.

Tom White and Tony Morris each recalled that on Saturday nights during drill weekends at Indiantown Gap, the Troop would often hold barracks parties. Upstairs, they would "swing the bucket," using a large enamel cauldron hung from the rafters. Downstairs, they would flood the latrine—a tiled room sunk three feet deep into the ground—by blocking its single drain to form a swimming pool. They would also hold "locker races," in which men would climb into wall lockers and ride them down the stairs and out the front door.

Annual training took place each year at either Fort Drum, New York, or at Camp Pickett, Virginia. During these two weeks of training, they would get the middle weekend off. This brief respite, called Middle Weekend, was celebrated with special gusto.

Middle Weekends at Fort Drum were often spent on the water. For example, according to the Troop's official history, in 1966, "the Troop commissioned a 90-passenger cruise ship, transformed it into a 'pirate frigate,' and enjoyed the sights of Alexandria Bay and the 1000 Islands. In spite of high-spirited passengers, the ship returned to shore intact."

When annual training was held at Camp Pickett, Troopers would always visit the Cavalier Hotel Virginia Beach. Having once been one of the better resorts on the East Coast, the Cavalier had seen better days by the time the Troop discovered it—and much worse days after each of their visits. Descending like an annual cloud locusts, Troopers ranging in years from college freshmen to late middle age would arrive on Friday night to kick off festivities that would culminate with a First Sergeant's Party on Saturday night.

Anticipating this party, Junior Troopers would arise bright and early on Saturday morning to canvass the beach, passing out engraved invitations to attractive women of all ages, inviting them back to the Cavalier. Throughout the day, they subjected the poor hotel to much wear and tear, acting more like rock stars than suburban gentry. They didn't necessarily intend to break furniture, remove doorframes from hinges, ruin whole floors with overflowing bathtubs, or crash through ceilings while commando crawling through the ventilation systems. Such things seemed to just happen spontaneously of their own accord.

By 5:00 p.m. on Saturday, just as the security staff were about to phone the police, the marauding Troopers would abruptly disappear from view, leaving the beach, pool, and hospitality suite eerily vacant. An hour later, they would reemerge freshly groomed and shaven, wearing blazers, neckties, and polished penny loafers to attend the First Sergeant's Party where, by tradition, first-year Troopers served dinner dressed as "waitresses" in bikinis with water balloons filling the tops.

Skit Night would follow dinner. The men would perform witty, uproarious, and quite nuanced Broadway musical parodies composed over the prior year. Many of these featured bawdy corruptions of the original namesake songs, with titles such as *My Fair Lady?* (posed as a question), *South Passaic,* (it was always easy to get laughs by making fun of New Jersey), and *I Am the Very Model of a Modern Day Degenerate* (based on Gilbert and Sullivan).

As well all know, in every field of human endeavor, there arise champions whose talents surpass all who came before them. Though it's hard to define one Troop song writer who stands above the rest (the Troop's talent pool for rollicking song writing has historically been very rich), the unit's "Shakespeare of Song," its "Beethoven of Bawd," must surely have been James Blunt, who served on the Active Roll for twenty years starting in 1966 and whose songs are still belted out in the Armory today.

When asked to reveal his song-writing methods, Blunt responded thusly: "I would borrow then-popular tunes, such as "Eleanor Rigby" by the Beatles and "Annie's Song," or "Thank God I'm a Country Boy" by John Denver. I would then write about particular Troopers who had done something odd, funny, or memorable that year. I always strove to write the lyrics in a way that was companionable to the mood and spirit as well as, importantly, the rhyming scheme of the original song. Thus, the opening line of my perverted iteration of "Annie's Song" becomes, 'You fill up my nostrils . . .' instead of Mr. Denver's 'You fill up my senses . . .' See? It's close, but it's definitely no cigar."

At the 1975 camp at Fort Drum, armed with writing pads, felt tips, and more than a few Schmidt's beers, Blunt wrote the perennial Troop favorite "Thank God I'm a City Boy," based on John Denver's "Thank God I'm a Country Boy," an original copy of which is photographed on the following page. As Blunt explains, "The refrain at once respects and rejects Mr. Denver's schmaltzy, down home lyrics about life on the farm entailing not a whole lot that a 'country boy can't hack.'"

The song premiered to an enthusiastic reception at skit night that year, and then took on unexpected momentum of its own. The following autumn, Trooper Ned Grassi attended a John Denver concert at Princeton University's Jadwin Gymnasium. When Denver cued up "Thank God I'm a Country Boy," Grassi jumped on stage and sang a contrapuntal Country Boy/City Boy version of the then wildly popular song. The audience loved the First City Troop version. Denver seemed to take it good-naturedly.

# City Boy

Tune  John Denver                    Lyrics: James Blunt                    Scrivener: Neil L

Well life in the city's full of wondrous things to do
Supping at the Barclay and perving at the zoo
Climb atop of Billy Penn and breathe in the view (count to 7)
Thank God I'm a city boy

Those country folk have some animals and tools
but I never have cottoned to those country bumpkin fools
When I play, I play by the Philadelphia rules (count to 7)
Thank god I'm a city boy

*Well, I got me a Beemer, I'm politic'ly right of middle
When the sun goes down, I got swordfish on the griddle
Life ain't bad when your middle name is Biddle (count to 7)
Thank God I'm a city boy**

Rowin' down the river past Boat House Row
Picnicking a Clivedon is the only way to go
A carriage ride to Valley Green when daylight's getting low (count to 7)
Thank God I'm a city boy.

Life in Chestnut Hill can really be fine
Tennis at the Pennlyn Club and knocking the Main Line
The bearnaise sauce at Blue Bell Inn is better than mine (count to 7)
Thank God I'm a city boy

CHORUS

*Young Troopers rummaging through overstuffed filing cabinets in the Armory cellar recently unearthed this ancient, blurry photocopy of James Blunt's musical masterpiece, "City Boy." Note Blunt's sporting reference to the rivalry between Chestnut Hill and the Main Line. [First City Troop collection]*

# Chapter 21

# Bicentennial Ball and Ride to Boston

In 1974, the Troop celebrated its Bicentennial with the same enthusiasm it had for the Centennial in 1874. Over 900 Troopers and their ladies converged on the Armory for a Bicentennial Ball which began at 11 p.m. following private dinner parties held throughout the Delaware Valley. In a drill hall transformed for the occasion, they danced through the night and well into the morning, with a brief interval for breakfast.

Sitting with friends that night, Rich Diffenderfer (having long since forgiven the Troop for pressing him into service) hopped up on the table and sang the "Draft Dodger Rag," a popular song at the time. The men around him lifted the table to shoulder high as he stood on it singing, so everyone in the hall could hear him. Years he later recalled with amazement, "They lifted the table up and set it back down so gently that not a drop of wine was spilled."

Preparations for the ball, which had been going on for months in advance, evidenced the usual mix of military precision and memorable mishap that always seem to characterize the Troop in action. A Junior Trooper tasked with ordering 200 boxes of matches mistakenly ordered 200 *cases* instead. A few days later, a wooden pallet arrived at the Armory stacked six feet high with enough matches for that ball—and for every social event since. To this day (in 2015), the Troop still has boxes of matches left over from that one pallet in 1974. If you ever visit the Armory and someone offers you a light from a book of matches with the Troop crest on it, you're smoking a piece of history.

*Matches in 2015 left over from the 1974 Bicentennial Ball. (Author's photo)*

Bicentennial celebrations were not limited to the great ball. In 1975, National Geographic photographer Ted Spiegel asked a group of Troopers the following question: "Would it be possible for you guys to retrace your first mission when you escorted General Washington on his way to assume command of the Continental Army in Boston in 1775?" He said it would make for a great story if the trip could be done on horseback and in 18th century uniforms. Embracing Spiegel's idea as a mandate, the Troopers spent the next three weeks mapping out Washington's original trip and contracting replicas of their original 1774 uniforms. On June 20th seventeen men departed from Independence Mall on horseback, aiming to arrive on Cambridge Commons by July 4 at exactly the spot where General Washington took command of the Continental Army.

After the first hour in the saddle, certain deficiencies in the 18th-century clothing became quite evident. As Dan Mannix recalled, "The britches were linen, which has no stretch, and we mistakenly placed stitches on the inside seams, which guaranteed them to rub and split. We also had wool jackets—perfect for the July weather." Upon reaching the Lambertville Inn in New Jersey, David Stokes's britches were so ripped that he had to improvise patches from some of the restaurant's white linen table napkins.

*Troopers kick off their commemorative ride north from Philadelphia to Boston in 1975, retracing the unit's first mission two centuries earlier. (From the Philadelphia Evening Bulletin Photograph Collection. Courtesy of the Special Collections Research Center, Temple University Libraries. Philadelphia, PA 19122)*

Amazingly, the logistics for this expedition relied primarily on the goodwill of horsey people up and down the Mid-Atlantic. The Troopers covered each day's ride on horses borrowed from friends and acquaintances they met along the way. As news of their journey spread ahead of them, people would appear to offer steeds, food, and lodging. The Troopers rarely knew from day to day where they would spend the night or whose horses they would ride. They simply rolled northward on the wave of patriotic fervor sweeping the East Coast as enthusiasm grew for the upcoming American Bicentennial.

Each day, they plodded along the same roads that Washington had followed, visiting the same inns and taverns that existed in his time. Conveniently, many of these were still in business, and because they had originally been built within a day's ride or walk of each other, it was natural to go from one to the next. Local hospitality was not without its limits. Although each subsequent town welcomed the incoming Troopers with open arms, the Troopers found themselves sleeping in firehouses or other public buildings and not in people's homes, because in addition to their 18th-century appearance, they gave off a strong 18th-century smell.

In Piermont, New York, they hitched a ride to New York City on folk singer Pete Seeger's sloop, *Clearwater.* On this leg of the trip, two centuries collided as Troopers in colonial dress bantered with female Seeger groupies on board, trying not to ogle as the coquettish hippies lounged around provocatively on railings and deck hatches in skimpy t-shirts and acutely cutoff jeans. Mannix later joked that Seeger would have flipped had he realized he was giving passage to a bunch of staunch Republicans.

Arriving in Manhattan to great fanfare, the Troopers mounted fresh horses and clippety-clopped down Wall Street to dine at Fraunces Tavern, reaching it on precisely the same day that Washington had 200 years earlier. They also ate the same period meal.

*Are they 18th-century cavalry scouts, or a 1960s rock band? Gentlemen of Gloucester hitch a ride on Pete Seeger's sloop, Clearwater. The hippie Seeger groupies sharing this passage are unfortunately absent from the photo. (First City Troop collection)*

They proceeded north to the Massachusetts Turnpike— still following Washington's exact route—which by 1975 was a six-lane freeway. As Mannix said, "We rode along the turnpike until we reached Exit 20, then we left the freeway and took a right." On July 2, 1975, twenty miles outside Boston, they hit a marker commemorating George Washington's original trip, which said, "On this day, July 2, 1775, at 2 p.m. General George Washington passed by here on his way to Boston to take command of the Continental Army." Eerily, just then Mannix glanced at his wristwatch and noticed that it was exactly 2 p.m.

When the Troopers finally reached Cambridge Commons, they met a cacophony of reenactors' musket and cannon fire that drove their rented horses crazy. David Stokes said, "To my surprise, after so many days on horseback, I had such a firm seat in the saddle that it felt impossible to get thrown." The journey finally ended that night with an 18th-century-styled ball attended by a throng of Massachusetts politicians and historical reenactors. A number of Troopers' wives drove up to accompany them to this event, naturally wearing their own period clothes. Troop bachelors brought dates from among the many camp followers who had attached themselves to the procession along the way.

While Active-roll members strove to promote the Troop with various escapades in the years following Vietnam, the older generation worked to keep other Philadelphia institutions relevant to the outside world.

For example, World War II veteran Elkins "Elkie" Wetherill (mentioned above in an anecdote about the Border Plate) focused his efforts in the 1960s and 70s on revamping the Philadelphia Stock Exchange to compete with the New York. He refined the Philadelphia Exchange by offering longer trading hours, faster transaction speeds, and by allowing multiple specialists to compete on any given stock—as opposed to the New York Stock Exchange practice of confining specialists into exclusive franchises. All of these innovations drove down Philadelphia Exchange prices. When New York refused to offer quantity discounts to large banks and mutual funds, Wetherill invited them to join his stocks exchange and forego dealing with a broker altogether. Wetherill's agitation led to a 1976 Securities & Exchange Commission ruling that forced New York's "Big Board" to abandon its 183-year-old price-fixing agreement requiring all members to charge the same price for brokerage services.

As a local man of affairs, Wetherill headed the Delaware Valley Regional Planning Commission, the Philadelphia Drama Guild, and he chaired the board at Philadelphia's Public TV station, WHYY. These business accomplishments were admirable, but what really made Wetherill one of the classic Gentlemen of Gloucester were his outside interests as a country squire. He balanced competitive business practices with an aesthetic taste for preserving the rural past. He was a superb horseman, and his devotion to land preservation led him to write *A Field Guide to Some of the Common Grasses of Southeastern Pennsylvania*, a book published by the Brandywine Conservancy.

# Chapter 22

# Performance in the Field

Although Troopers certainly put a great deal of energy into festivities, they were not lax in their military duties. Indeed, it's the cavalryman's custom to both work and play hard. Sometimes they scored low ratings from outside evaluators, but more often they tended to exceed National Guard training standards.

Hugh Reddit, who enlisted in 1973 and eventually became squadron commander, once observed that in the field, First City Troopers tended to be "tactically proficient and technically absent." When I begged him to elaborate this intriguing turn of phrase, he said, "Our men were clever, but they were generally disinterested in technicalities or military nomenclature. There was one First Sergeant, for example, who was very talented as an administrator. Under his leadership, the men scored excellent ratings in almost every testing area. But I wouldn't be surprised if, for years, he never fired a weapon himself, or if he never knew how to operate a tank! He was good enough at coordinating everyone else's talents that no one thought to ask. He always knew how to spread the guys with technical know-how throughout the unit, so they could raise the standards of everyone else."

Reddit continued, "But when it came to tactics, the same Troopers who seemed impervious to technical details could be brilliant at improvising solutions to field problems." At one annual training exercise, regular army evaluators were impressed by the unit's performance of a complicated field maneuver called "Route Reconnaissance and Withdraw to Supplementary Defensive Positions." They called it, "The best overall performance of these missions in ten years, with aspects of it the best we've ever seen."

*Troop leaders discuss tactics at annual training in the early 1980s. (Troop History: 1948-1991)*

David Biddle Stokes and Bruce Maxfield were two Troopers who helped carry the unit both tactically and technically. Son of Honorary Captain William Stanley Stokes, David served in the regular army before joining the Troop. He explained, "My dad was in the chain of command at squadron. So, when I came of military age, I didn't want to join the Troop as daddy's little boy." Stokes joined the Army in 1967 and spent three years in Germany working with Pershing missiles. After that—and a yearlong trip through Africa from Tangiers to Cape Town during which he drove a customized Land Rover and hunted animals along the way—he returned home to join the Troop.

His best friend, Bruce Maxfield, joined at the same time, having also served in the regular army. In Vietnam, Maxfield ran clandestine operations nets in II Corps, Laos & Cambodia. To confirm intelligence, he would plan operations with Long Range Recon Patrol teams (LRRPs). He said, "Their job was to get me in and get me out." In light of these experiences, Maxfield took National Guard's training standards quite seriously. He said, "Serving two tours in Vietnam taught me that inexperience will kill you and experience used carelessly will get you killed too. I used my perspective on weapon systems, tactics, and strategic/covert operations planning to help improve the Troop's field performance at annual training."

*Bruce Maxfield's tank crew breaks for happy hour at annual training. Just after this photo was taken, a visiting range officer called them "decadent" for eating smoked cheese and oysters in the field. (Photo from Thomas Boyle)*

From year to year, the Troop's performance ebbed and flowed depending on its leadership quality. After a stretch of abysmal performance in the 1970s, Captain Alexander Kerr tightened things up considerably in the end of that decade. In 1978 and 1979, training evaluators from the 82nd Airborne were fascinated by the Troop's cohesion and its ability to draw synergies from the Active Roll's varied prior-service backgrounds.

Here's an odd example: at tank ranges, gunners with Navy experience tended to shoot much better than gunners who only had Army training. Why? As Roy West explained, "Shooting 40-millimeter Bofors cannon and five-inch naval guns at sea made operating tank guns easy." In addition to things like that, First Troop tank crews typically stayed together for five years or more at a stretch—much longer than tank crews in active duty units. This gave them time to learn each other's quirks, strengths, and weaknesses, and to operate as one man.

At annual training in 1985, another tank crew decided to speak French in order to confound enemy forces listening in on their radio traffic. They stitched together a blue, white, and red French tricolor flag, attached it to their radio antenna and spent war games week speaking only French both in the tank and over the radio—much to the confusion of their regular army evaluators. Their "flag" remains framed on a wall in the Armory today.

*Tank fire at night in the early 1980s. Troop tank crews spent years training together, learning each other's quirks, strengths, and weaknesses. In one tank, the commander and gunner were both equally dyslexic. Each had a tendency to confuse right from left. Whenever the commander wanted his gunner to swing the turret to the left, he would mistakenly tell him to swing right. The gunner would instantly swing left, thinking it was right. But the system worked. (Photo from Thomas Boyle)*

*Capturing unit's whimsical yet practical spirit, Trooper Daniel Ott displays the Mickey Mouse wristwatch with alligator band and compass that he wore during his Active Roll years. Although run over by a car once, it still works. (Author's photo)*

Come fair weather or foul, many a Trooper considered himself a man of action, ready to mount the breach in times of emergency. During a drill weekend in 1983, a severe blizzard hit Philadelphia that shut the city down and prevented National Guard units across the state from training. Troopers Mitch Harding and William "Bucky" Buchanan made it to the Armory that day, however—because they happened to be living in the building (in a bachelor apartment that warrants its own separate story).

As the flurries drifted down that quiet morning, Buchanan's glance fell upon a brand new, turbo-charged APC (Armored Personnel Carrier) which the Troop had just acquired from a unit in Texas. He sidled up to Captain Dennis Boylan and asked for permission to take the new vehicle out for a test drive, and to survey the shutdown city. Boylan waved him away in half-agreement.

Bucky and Harding charged up the vehicle and lurched out of the Armory into the snow. A block down the road, they noticed a car stuck in the snow and towed it out for them. The owners thanked them heartily which gave Buchanan the chance to shrug ostentatiously and dismiss the matter as "all in a day's work."

Our Troopers progressed deeper into the city. When they reached Independence Hall, they discovered a KYW News Radio van helplessly spinning its tires in a snow bank and duly set it free. Buchannan invited the newscasters into the back of the APC for a nip of Old Granddad (to ward off the cold). The newscasters responded by broadcasting footage of the dashing Troopers on live television.

Their appetite for good deeds much whetted by this unexpected publicity (and further swigs of Old Grandad), Harding and Buchanan continued exploring snow-hushed Philadelphia, searching for more people to save. According to Buchanan (recalling the event thirty years later), the following message then blared on his radio: "I95 has been shut down by snow! *Can you please go down there and save the city?*" They responded immediately, executing a grand sweep from Route 676 to I-95, saving people right and left along the way. When they finally tired from all this heroism, they returned to the Armory bursting with pride in a job well done.

Instead of getting pats on the back, however, they faced court martial. Because Philadelphia's entire metropolitan population had nowhere to go that morning, and since there were few other channels on television at the time, images of Buchanan (standing in the track commander's hatch clad in a Troop campaign hat and brightly colored ski jacket) reached a much broader regional audience than would have normally been expected—including high ranking officers in the both the Pennsylvania and New Jersey National Guard.

An Inspector General investigation sought to charge the Troopers for using gasoline and abusing government property, but they ultimately found no legal grounds for prosecution. Ten years later, however, when the Blizzard of 1996 paralyzed the city, the PA National Guard mobilized local units as soon as the snow fell. According to Buchanan, "the private mission they tried to hang us for in '83 became the new Standard Operating Procedure (SOP) for responding to blizzards."

*William "Bucky" Buchanan in his 113 Armored Personnel Carrier. (Troop History: 1948-1991)*

## Chapter 23

# Farewell to the Richmond Blues

Ever since World War I, the Troop has struggled to strike a balance between staying relevant as a modern military organization while also retaining its "ancient rights and privileges" as one of America's oldest private, independent, and volunteer societies.

*Honorary Captain Dennis Boylan describes the battle rings on the Troop's guidon to guests from the John Jay Institute in the Armory's Officers' Club. (Photo by Andrew Colket)*

In 1978, Lieutenant Dennis Boylan aided this effort when he got the United States Army to officially acknowledge the Troop as the only company-sized unit with federal permission to carry its own battle standard. This might seem like a minor detail, but it was actually a big deal. Under normal circumstances, only units of battalion or higher size (1000 soldiers or more) are permitted that honor.

In 1985, the Troop inched another step forward when it won the right to have its own distinctive unit crest—an honor which was also for company-sized elements.

Around that time, the Troop also received permission to carry seventeen battle rings on the staff of its guidon (a small flag that cavalry troops carry)—the most carried by any military unit in the United States.

Other units weren't so fortunate. Although the Troop may be the last unit of its type serving in the United States today, until the 1970s, it had a rival—the Richmond Light Infantry Blues.

Formed in 1793—seventeen years *after* the Troop—the Richmond Blues once maintained a fine Virginian heritage. When the other ancient American militia units dropped from active service throughout the twentieth century, the Richmond Blues were the only ones who kept the flame alive with First City. With such similar backgrounds the Blues and the Troop had a rocky, love-hate relationship. At annual training throughout the 1960s, they were often pitted against each other in war games, vying tooth and claw in the ruthless struggle for supremacy among East Coast "champagne" units.

The Troop's official records from this period are rich in the language of struggle. In 1969, we read, "the Richmond Blues seemed anxious to renew the War Between the States, and several of their members made track vehicle turn-in very difficult for the Troop... At Hughie's Breakfast, when the Troop returned to Philadelphia, the Captain was presented with the complete camouflage uniform of Captain Bailey, the commanding officer of the Richmond Blues."

The next year, still peeved at the "less than cordial" reception accorded by the Richmond Blues the previous year, the Troop embraced war games with special vigor. With much effort, the Troop made "such an impressive showing that [the Blues] were thrown into disarray resulting in their commander being relieved from the field."

*First City Troopers host the Richmond Blues in Philadelphia for General Washington's birthday dinner in 1970.*

Off the field of battle, all was politeness and good sportsmanship. Part of this affinity was doubtless helped by a deep-seated Philadelphian affection for other regions that formed the original Thirteen Colonies, with special honor given to the Tidewater South and coastal Yankeedom. The Blues and the Troop respected each other well enough to celebrate George Washington's birthday together at the Armory in 1970.

Sadly, membership numbers in the Blues started to decline at the end of the 1970s. They sent delegates to Philadelphia to see what pointers they could learn about long term survival. Why? Because Philadelphia institutions of all stripes—especially the tiny ones you never hear about—have an amazing knack for pragmatically enduring over very long stretches of time. But there was little that could be done.

According to some Troopers who remember those visits, the Blues had an unbending aristocratic streak that the Troop intentionally avoided. They were unwilling to shape-shift, to adapt to changes that were occurring in the National Guard. William Buchanan attributed the Troop's flexibility to a hidden Quaker predilection for bottom-up consensus-seeking as opposed to top-down decision making. The Blues' demise may also have been due to the fact that Richmond had a smaller population pool from which to draw new members. At any rate, Troopers lamented the Blues' demise as much as they did.

*The Troop was once one of several posh "champagne" units that existed in a number of American cities. Some of these remain in existence today as social clubs, but all except the Troop have ceased performing active military service. In this 1870s German illustration of swank American units, a Richmond Blues soldier stands third from the left, while a First City Trooper stands on the far right. (From a pamphlet titled* Die Armee der Vereinigten Staaten von Amerika, *donated by Vinson Nash)*

# Chapter 24

# 1984 Troop Daughters Ball

As you may have gathered thus far in our story, the ball has been one of the Troop's preferred forms of social celebration over the centuries.

According to Nathaniel Burt, "A Philadelphian away at a stuffy party found himself rather desperately describing to a deaf partner the glories of the City Troop. He enlarged on their customs and costumes, their helmets and tight pants. 'And,' he found himself shouting during a sudden lapse in conversation elsewhere, 'they have the most magnificent *balls*.'."

Balls have special attraction for gentlemen-soldiers because they engage such military skills as strategic planning, logistics, bringing supplies and personnel to bear on a set time and date for maximum dramatic impact, vibrant uniforms (both for men and women), risk of casualty (social gaffes, dancefloor injuries, fights and scraps due to overdrinking or romantic jilting), and promise of reward.

Reflecting on the whirl of activities at such affairs, the Duke of Wellington said, "The history of a battle is not unlike the history of a ball. Some individuals may recollect all the little events of which the great result is the battle won or lost, but no individual can recollect the order in which, or the exact moment at which, they occurred."

The most impressive ball in living memory was the great Troop Daughters Ball of 1984, which featured all the hallmarks described above.

Planning for it began 18 years earlier, when 11 Troop families gave birth to baby daughters in 1966. Excited to have so many daughters at once, they formed a committee to finance a massive bash for the girls when they would all come of debutante age. Each family agreed to pay $500 to $800 annually for 18 years, so that by 1984 they would have $99,000 with which to entertain all their friends and relations free of charge.

This plan worked well enough—for a while. That is, until some of the more flamboyant Troopers plunged their working capital into AT&T warrants which soon tanked, taking most of the debutante money with it. "Cooler heads were clearly required," explains Charlie Meredith, "so the wives stepped in."

Nell Grim, a Wellesley-and Harvard-educated self-taught manager of her own private portfolio, recommended a selection of boring, safe, and winning ideas that ultimately won the day. According to Larry Grim, "By 1984 we had all the money we needed and more. We overbought for the ball in almost every way, which allowed us to declare 'liquid dividends' liquor, wine, and other stuff for the partners."

But, to quote Wellington again, it was a near-run thing. For years Nell had to stave off investment suggestions from swashbuckling Troopers bursting with get-rich-quick schemes. One of them wanted to stock up cases of expensive wine to store in caves. Another wanted to buy shares in Klouff Gold

Mining Company, whose motto was "Through the Roof with Klouff!"

To foster esprit de corps among the girls during the years leading up to the ball, their parents gathered them together at periodic parties, each having its own whimsical theme. As Alix Davis Cummin recalled, "there was a Gong Show theme, a skateboarding theme (it was the 1970s), a rock concert theme. And one time we toured Bucks County in double-decker bus from London." Larry Grim, a country lawyer gifted with a flair for overstatement, gentle ribbing, and onomatopoeia, wrote minutes for these events that still make his friends laugh today.

In order to strike just the right musical tone, several Troopers persuaded high-society bandleader Lester Lanin to play the event. World famous for his long, smooth, jazzy, poppy, upbeat medleys, he played for European royalty and at the White House. His astronomical fees would have busted Nell Grim's budget, but Lanin had a soft spot for Philadelphia, having grown up there, and an amused affection for the Troop. As Peter Clauss said, "Lanin never forgot his local roots! He told us he could easily command $50,000 for a debutante ball in New York or Houston, but for Philadelphians, he offered to do it for $10,000."

On ball night, December 29, 1984, 1,400 people streamed into the Armory after dining at private clubs and restaurants around town. It was warm enough that evening for the young ladies to arrive in open cars. The event kicked off at 11 p.m. and lasted until dawn, with a pause for breakfast at 3 a.m. Whistling in retrospect, Clauss said, "When the secondary-school-aged invitees sought their parent's approval to attend the ball, scores of parents flipped out when they saw the event's start time. One of them said, 'what the hell kind of party for kids starts at 11 p.m.!?'" Clauss tried to placate them, explaining that the ball was a full-family event for ages ranging from children to grandparents.

When the dust settled 24 hours later, everyone agreed that the ball had been a raging success. Jim Blunt commemorated it with a Troop song to the tune of *Oceana Roll*, a catchy ragtime number much loved at the Orpheus Club. The event even accomplished its medieval mating purposes. As Clauss said, "Lots of romances came out of it, and quite a few marriages."

According to local lore, the 1984 Daughters Ball resurrected a debutante tradition which had seemed doomed to extinction a decade earlier. The country had changed dramatically between when the daughters were born in 1966 and when they came of age in 1984. By that time, the spirt of the 1960s and 70s had run its course in America, and the Reagan Revolution coincided with a nostalgic yearning that swept the country. The debutante tradition, which had seemed passé for a while, was re-embraced as a cherished link to the past. *Town & Country* and *Esquire* magazines each featured stories about the Troop ball, and six years later, Whit Stillman's film *Metropolitan* celebrated such events from the New York perspective.

Troopers now hold a debutante ball whenever enough members have daughters of similar age to warrant one. Just this year (2015) a number of baby girls were born to Troopers, which means that they will start saving their pennies for an event in 2033.

*The 1984 Daughters Ball led to a number of Trooper marriages. (Troop History: 1948-1991) The Schoettle wedding photo (below) actually dates from 1976.*

# Chapter 25

# The Fraternity Era

Not only did the 1984 ball lead to Troop romances, it attracted new recruits. Perry Gresh said, "I had no interest in sports or in joining the military, but I was so jealous of all the guys in uniform at the '84 Troop Ball that I felt compelled to take part myself." He enlisted in the Army and remained on the Active Roll for the following two decades.

Gresh was part of a new wave of young men who signed up in the 1980s for fraternal reasons. His cousin George Coates, who joined up with him, said, "The Troop seemed like a great way to build friendships. Although I'm in various Philadelphia clubs and associations today, out of my ten best friends, eight are Troopers." When Coates went to basic training, the only physical activities he had embraced up to that point in life had been shooting, sailing, and riding. "I considered backgammon a team sport!" he laughed. He enjoyed how the army broadened his social horizons. "Having grown up in a Main Line bubble, I loved the chance to mix with people from other backgrounds. My bunk mate was a crazy Cajun from rural Louisiana. We got along swimmingly and kept in touch for years afterward."

The Troop attracted many of its members from the University of Pennsylvania. Nick Bowden discovered the unit in 1986 while studying math and finance at Penn. As a shy young man, who he felt like he was drowning in big-city campus anonymity, he wanted to build friendships by joining a fraternity. But after visiting a number of student organizations, he found their focus on fellowship without sacrifice to be hollow.

At a St. Elmo's party, he met David Thayer, a Wharton student who had just joined the Troop. Bowden visited the unit and fell in love with the idea of serving his country with academic peers. The prospect of going through Basic Training seemed scary at the time, but took the plunge and went to Fort Knox. On some nights at Fort Knox, he cried himself to sleep, thinking "What have I done to my life!?" But he hardened up to army life and eventually became a First Sergeant.

Bowden recalls that a popular Penn professor, E. Digby Baltzell, spoke highly about the Troop in his lectures. A sociologist whose chronicles of the American Protestant Establishment popularized the term WASP (White Anglo Saxon Protestant), Baltzell believed that the American ruling class had betrayed the nation in the 1960s when it started losing its self-imposed stoicism, and when it refused to include newcomers from other ethnicities. (New York Times columnist David Brooks has since picked up Baltzell's mantel with such op-ed pieces as *Why Our Elites Stink*, a lamentation about character traits lost since the decline of the Protestant Establishment.) According to Jason Mayland, a Trooper who knew Baltzell, the professor saw the Troop as an ideal way to blend new money and old money, new blood and blood, into a uniquely American form of gentleman.

As the Cold War flared up in the 1980s, the regular Army formalized, centralized, and intensified National Guard leadership-training in ways that forced Troopers seeking promotion to devote more and more time each year to Army training schools. Perversely, this barred the very Troopers with

183

the most administrative potential—the lawyers, bankers, and general executives—from becoming military leaders. They simply couldn't take that much time off work.

In response, the Troop chose to elect occasional younger men to the Active Roll with the understanding that they would get fast-tracked to become officers immediately upon joining. This required a delicate social contract in which the would-be leader would postpone his civilian career for a while to focus on the Troop, and in return, mature Troopers would help him professionally later in life.

Treading such territory was quite hazardous (potentially even cancerous) from a cultural perspective. For two centuries, the Troop prided itself on vetting its members through long years in the lowest ranks. Everyone feared that men fast-tracked for leadership roles would not have time to absorb the understanding of what it meant to be a gentleman-private—to feel it in his bones.

Keith Rogers was the test monkey (I use the term respectfully) for this new procedure. In 1983 he joined the Troop while already enrolled in ROTC (Reserve Officers' Training) at college. Because he knew he was bucking an important Troop custom, he walked humbly, electing to wear E1 (private) insignia on his uniform instead of the E5 (sergeant) rank to which he was entitled.

Like other junior Troopers, he threw himself into the equestrian program, and made the Troop his main priority in life. He said, "Throughout my 20s, I devoted that entire decade to serving in the Troop. I didn't get married until much later. Aside from work, I made the Troop my sole focus in life. But since the Troop had so much to offer socially, it was a satisfying focus."

Just as Rogers joined with his intention to immediately become an officer, other Troopers chose early on to become senior NCOs (Non-commissioned Officer) someday, and to never accept a commission. Alexander Bevin Cummin, whose father Jerry had been a Troop Captain, preferred to be an NCO because NCOs remained in their home units long after officers were promoted elsewhere. Stealing a phrase from the French Foreign Legion, he said, "The Troop is my home."

During his twenty-year tenure, Cummin spent many weeks at military schools working to become First Sergeant. Like many Troop NCOs, his manner was a curious blend of gruffness and refinement. As an Episcopal Academy and University of Pennsylvania man, he often wore a blazer and bowtie, and his speech—though rich in requisite profanity— was more often peppered with tennis and sailing analogies and French phrases in the correct accent. In the field, he would smoke cigars stored in a humidor home-made from a .50 caliber ammo can lined with cedar.

By the mid-1980s, the Troop's "wild years" approached their end. The National Guard eliminated middle weekend from its training calendar and —with a pen stroke—erased the annual event which had produced the Troop's rowdiest behavior. The party element remained strong, but grew milder throughout the 1990s. The magnificent skit night tradition almost died along with middle weekend. But just as Trooper's culinary customs refused to die when the mess section disbanded, their urge to sing carried on in the form of an annual Songmeister competition. At this event, which continues today, participants perform newly written bawdy songs before a panel composed of Captain, First Sergeant, and a bunch of jeering, hooting, and hollering fellow Troopers. The winner receives a loving cup which he gets to keep for the following year.

# Chapter 26

# The NCO Club

The Troop's armory building has gone through many transitions since its construction in 1901. The largest of these occurred when the unit switched from horses to mechanized vehicles after World War II. Throughout the 50s, 60s and 70s, the building was treated as the rough and ready home of a volunteer cavalry unit. Its general maintenance often reflected the dingy, threadbare condition of Philadelphia at the time.

By degrees however, it was refined and upgraded as well. The old hayloft was converted into a museum in the late 1960s, to give a formal home to all the antiques and hand-me-downs collected from deceased honorary Troopers and their families over the years. Although the building was primarily a military installation, it also functioned as a social hub. This dual use had much in common with volunteer fire departments in rural America.

Like many august institutions, the Armory's NCO Club, "a tree fort for grownups," had small beginnings. In the late 1960s some enterprising Troop NCOs spiffed up a cramped storage space on the mezzanine floor with paneling left over from various home-improvement projects. Few of these panels matched. When they were nailed to the wall, so many variations of plywood laminate were in evidence that the room was nicknamed "The Paneling Museum."

NCOs originally ruled this inner sanctum with a rod of iron. They financed further improvements to the joint through fines humorously levied on hapless privates. As one man recalled, "When I was a Junior Trooper, we would always take an extra $25 to drill weekends with the expectation of being fined for such trumped up infractions as standing in a sergeant's shadow or telling a bad joke. If you told a joke and the NCO was able to remain straight-faced, he'd say 'Not funny. That'll be $5.'"

Josh West, whose father Roy would bring him to the Armory as a child to play on the tanks, said, "The old NCO Club was like the dive bar at a volunteer firehouse, stocked with Rolling Rock beer and rotgut booze. An old-fashioned cathode-ray TV set hung from the ceiling on a piece of plywood, suspended by chains. Some people loved that the place was a dump because they came from such pristine surroundings at home, and most NCOs had memberships at the best clubs in Philadelphia anyway. When they wanted a decent place to hold the monthly sergeants' meeting, they would have dinner at Merion or Philly Cricket." (Merion Cricket Club and Philadelphia Cricket Club are located on opposite sides of the Schuylkill River, on the Main Line and in Chestnut Hill, respectively. To make driving times equitable, Troopers alternated their events between "both sides of the river.")

It eventually rankled some of the NCOs that their club room was so squalid compared to the nicely appointed Officers' Club on the other side of the building, which had a vaulted ceiling, antique furniture, and numerous 18th century paintings. Because all Troopers are considered socially equal, the Officers Club would regularly open its doors to all ranks, but the keys to the room still belonged to the "Os."

For years, the officers half-heartedly promised to finance improvements to the NCO Club, but they always procrastinated. Finally, Harvard-educated and cavalry-mustachioed Stockton Illoway (considered by many to be the most effective First Sergeant in living memory) got fed up with the delay. On his last day as First Sergeant, he found a sledgehammer and smashed up the entire NCO Club—walls, fixtures, and all—damaging the place beyond repair. He then walked down to Captain Keith Rogers's office, knocked gently on the door and said, "Sir, you guys will have to fix the NCO Club." Rogers took a look at the demolished room and responded swiftly. With financial help from Peter Hamilton (a generous Trooper who helped the unit many times over the years), men of all ranks worked in relays around the clock to rebuild the place by hand. Within weeks, the Troop found itself with a handsomely appointed NCO Club which—for the first time ever—was fit for entertaining outside guests.

*The Second NCO Club, built by Troopers (including the Captain) with their own hands while working around the clock in relays. With an open bar and no closing time, it was a hive of activity morning and night. (Photo from Howard Wisch, Jr.)*

189

# Chapter 27

# Annual Troop Cruise

Over the generations, Troopers have added and subtracted numerous customs and events from the annual roster which have fallen beyond the narrow ramifications of military service and horse riding. Among the more recent of these is the annual Troop Cruise.

It started sometime in the 1980s or 90s when a number of Troopers sailing boats on the Chesapeake happened upon each other unexpectedly. In the one boat were older men, and in the other were younger men, but when they noticed that each other's boats were flying Troop flags, they rafted up for a visit. After that, they decided to organize their chance meeting into a new tradition.

*The annual Troop Cruise. (Photo by Andrew Colket)*

Although the Troop Cruise is a much beloved event, perhaps the less that is said about it, the better. Sailing in boats may well be the natural complement to riding on horses, but the Troop's maritime record would suggest otherwise. Troop Cruise lore is replete with slap-stick incidents of nautical mishap—uproariously funny in the re-telling—often best left for internal consumption. The most treasured of these is the saga of the brass yacht cannon.

Peter Cachion grimaces painfully as he recalls the antique brass-and-mahogany yacht cannon ritually used to start the Troop Cruise. Firing a blank 12-gauge shotgun shell, when detonated from close range it sounded as loud as a real cannon. At the start of the cruise one year, Cachion carefully balanced this beautiful contraption on the stern of his friend's motor launch and pulled the ripcord. With a loud report, the racers were off... and so was the cannon! At that precise instant, Cachion realized (too late) that he should have braced it with his foot before firing. The hapless Trooper could only look in stunned horror as the cannon, obeying the immutable law of recoil, launched itself overboard and straight into the Chesapeake Bay. Cruelly, he endured one mocking second as he beheld a beautiful flash of sunlight reflecting from the cannon barrel as it plunged away from sight. The artillery piece was never recovered and continues to haunt him from the bottom of the Chesapeake to this day. Within five years, another Trooper brought a similar yacht cannon (borrowed from a friend who had just received it as a wedding gift) to start the Troop cruise, and to his deep chagrin, he repeated Cachion's mistake. Doubled over in laughter while describing the incident, Cachion claimed, "Once is a mistake. Twice is a catastrophe. But if it happens again, it will become a tradition!"

# Chapter 28

# First Deployment in Fifty Years

On September 11, 2001, Josh West switched on the TV to watch the morning news as he dressed for work. To his astonishment, the World Trade Center was on fire from a jet that had slammed into the North Tower. "What a terrible tragedy," he sighed, as he carried on with his morning routine. But then, as he left the house, his father shouted out the window that a second plane had just plunged into the other tower. "One plane crash may be an accident," thought Josh, "but two are an attack!"

Bursting with adrenaline, he tucked a .45 caliber pistol into his belt, threw a 12-gauge shotgun and a Ruger Mini 14 rifle into the trunk of his car, and drove to the Armory with the urgency of a Minuteman rushing to the village green at Lexington or Concord.

At the NCO Club, he found other Troopers also arriving—Philadelphia Minutemen, dressed in Brooks Brothers attire, and *armed to the teeth*! For the rest of the morning, they watched the news and telephoned friends to see what was going on around the country.

West's cell phone rang with an urgent call from Logan Fenstermacher, an A-Troop NCO who lived out in rural Pennsylvania. Fenstermacher had been stocking military supplies for years, waiting for some catastrophe to occur in which he could put his preparedness to use. Unable to contain his excitement, he shouted, "Lt. West, I just saw the news and am on my way! What should I bring!?" Equally enthused, West roared back, "Glad you called! Get your ass down here and bring everything you got!"

Three hours later, Fenstermacher's van screeched into drill hall, laden with various weapons, equipment, and 11,000 rounds of 5.56 ammunition (for M16 rifles) and 6,000 rounds of 7.62 (for machine guns). The National Guard had not been officially activated, but true to their colonial roots, the First City Troop was armed and ready.

Everyone braced for what might come next.

The common sentiment was, "Is this the beginning of a nation-wide coordinated attack?" Philadelphia had tall buildings too, you know. Maybe not as tall as all those mammoths in Manhattan, but tall enough to be hit by rogue airplanes! News came that Washington, D.C. had also been hit. Some Troopers wondered if the bastards might attack one of Philadelphia's many icons, like Independence Hall or the Liberty Bell. Expecting to see large buildings blowing up around him at any minute, one Trooper stood watch on the Armory roof all day with a radio and binoculars.

West, who described himself as having been in a state of "hyper-vigilance," phoned the Philadelphia Parking Authority and demanded that they tow all the cars parked near the Armory to form a cordon on 24th Street. The Parking Authority, equally alarmed, readily agreed. West then insisted that they block off 23rd Street as well, but they told him that to block up two arteries through that section of Rittenhouse would be overdoing it.

At the next Troop business meeting, a charming thing occurred. Captain Eric Guenther stood up and produced a large sheet of paper, the same size as a broadsheet that Trooper Jonathan Dunlap might have had at his print shop in 1776. Printed in florid language, it declared that the Troop would serve the Governor of Pennsylvania however, whenever, and wherever needed. One by one, each man in the room walked up to the Captain's table and signed the document with all the solemnity of the original Gentlemen of Gloucester who first mustered at Carpenters' Hall. Guenther then sealed it and sent it to the Adjutant General in Harrisburg.

Now there was nothing to do but wait.

The 9/11 terrorist attacks and subsequent United States actions in Afghanistan and Iraq occurred just as the U.S. military was re-thinking the role of the Army Reserve and the National Guard. For the first time since World War II, the Army deemed the Guard and Reserve as "operational" rather than "strategic" components. Therefore, they could now deploy them globally and not just domestically.

In March 2002, the 28th Infantry Division notified Captain Guenther that the Troop would be sent to Germany within three months for its first deployment in fifty years. Most people familiar with the Troop were astounded to hear this news, and many thought it was a joke. Others saw it as an opportunity to travel abroad.

Stable Sergeant Richard Walkup and his wife Jean immediately set to work drawing up plans to rent a vacant chateau, so they and other Troop families could bring their children to Europe while the menfolk were doing "army stuff." The Walkups were already homeschooling their kids on a horse farm in Chester County, so the move to a draftier country house in France or Germany wouldn't make much difference. Some of the Troop wives were school teachers, so educating the kids would be a snap.

Just as they were warming up to this magnificent plan, the phonograph needle screeched. Squadron sent word that instead of going to Germany, the Troop would now be sent to Bosnia. "Bosnia?!" went the collective gasp. This was most unwelcome news. During the 1990s, Bosnia had been in the news constantly as a war zone. It was front-burner media fodder. Officially, it was classified into the more mild sounding "hostile fire zone," but that still wasn't the sort of place where you could rent a castle and homeschool the kids.

Opinion was split among Troop wives about whether this was a noble thing to embrace, or a diabolical one to resist. Rebecca Guenther, a birthright Quaker, was very upset that her husband Eric might have to bear arms in combat. She had tolerated the Troop for years, because she sort of dismissed it as an organized means of men playing army. But how could she face it morally now as a pacifist Quaker? To address these questions, she threw herself into researching the whole Bosnia crisis. After reading many books and journalistic articles, she came to feel—by degrees—that the Troop's peacekeeping mission—to help people ravaged by war—would align closely with her Quaker beliefs. From then on, she was all support.

Alix Cummin, whose husband Bevin was a platoon sergeant, embraced the Bosnia deployment with gusto from the start. Her family had always embraced the idea of military service. Her father was a Trooper. As a young girl, her dad would let her ride on tanks at Fort Indiantown Gap during family visits. The way she saw it, "A lot of people give lip service to community, but it takes a stronger dimension when community is done in uniform. I was happy to see how many Troopers matured when they were called to Bosnia. It was gratifying to watch them evolve from party boys in the 1980s and 1990s to disciplined soldiers after 9/11. They'd always owned the social piece. But now they owned the Army piece."

Older Non-active and Honorary Troopers grappled with a range of feelings. Some of them—thrilled to see the unit put to military use after so many decades in mothballs—sprang up to organize a home support network to help deploying soldiers' families. Others urged active Troopers to avoid going, the way many of them had evaded Vietnam.

Joseph Seymour, who joined the unit while still in college, recalled meeting a Vietnam-era Trooper at the Armory one afternoon who said, "Man, that sucks you guys are getting deployed! So what are your plans to scamper away from it?" Annoyed at the man's use of the word "scamper," Seymour flared with anger and said, "Dude, you don't understand, do you?! We joined this unit to serve, and we have every intention of going!" But the man didn't seem to get it.

Kevin Harper, who joined the Troop in 1999, reacted to news about the deployment in light of his experiences on 9/11. When turned on the news and saw the second airplane crash into the World Trade Center, he realized that he had originally been scheduled to be on that very flight, but a job interview had forced him to cancel his plans and buy tickets on another airline. Having cheated death so closely, he wanted to take the fight back to the Middle East. He said, "I saw our being sent to Bosnia as an insult! I wanted to go to Afghanistan, to the fight back to the enemy. I thought, 'This won't be a real deployment.

We'll just be freeing other soldiers so they can do the real work.'"

Many Troopers whose enlistments were just about to expire faced a moral crisis. For example, Edward Ware and Edward Kellogg were just getting out of the National Guard and were under no obligation to re-enlist. But they each had family ties to the unit (Ware through his godfather and Kellogg through his father) that made them agonize over the right thing to do. After an all-night discussion, Kellogg decided he would reenlist and Ware decided he would not. But within days, each changed his mind.

When newly wedded Kellogg broached the issue with his wife, she insisted that he remain home. Ware on the other hand, finding no such excuses because he was unmarried, felt duty-bound to re-up. He wrenched himself from a lucrative job at Zürich Capital Markets, telling a friend, "I've played Army all these years, but now's the time to actually do it!" Although Ware's decision forced him to give up a six-figure income and future promotions at the firm, he said "I wouldn't take the money even [if it happened again] today. I wouldn't have forgiven myself for staying home during the Troop's first deployment in a lifetime." Once known as a First Troop party boy par excellence, Ware would transform himself into the quintessential "squared away" staff sergeant in Bosnia.

As debates about the up-coming deployment swirled around the Armory, the men grappled with philosophical questions that would seem absurd in any other unit.

For example, should they donate any of their drill pay while abroad? Since the 18th century, Troopers had always served voluntarily, donating money they earned from the Army into a common unit fund. Normally this money was used to boost the food budget, but it also went toward buying fancy weapons and other state of the art equipment unavailable to other militia units. When the matter came to a vote during a Monday night meeting, the Gentlemen of Gloucester relented and agreed that when deployed outside the United States, each man could keep all of his pay.

At initial entry processing, the on-duty JAG (Judge Advocate General) officer grew puzzled as private after private stepped into his office declaring income and assets at levels far surpassing anything he had seen before, even among officers. As Trooper Jason Mayland recalled, "When I sat down with the JAG, he asked, 'Do you have an estate of $500,000 or more?' I said, 'Of course.' He said 'You're the twenty-seventh man to say that today! Who *are* you people?' I said 'Sir, we're the First Troop Philadelphia City Cavalry.'"

A visiting Philadelphia newswoman interviewed Kevin Harper, who at age 28 had just hit his professional stride as an investment manager. Asked how much pay he would now earn as a Private First Class in comparison to his former civilian income, he deadpanned, "Less than one tenth." The otherwise chipper young reported was speechless.

At every turn, First Troop eccentricities—which had seemed perfectly normal on drill weekends and summer camp the previous year—raised soldiers' eyebrows from other units. When off duty, some could be spotted wandering around wearing polo shirts, seersucker, and Nantucket red. Some would play croquet on the lawn between the barracks. Others would gather to watch old BBC miniseries like *Brideshead Revisited* and *Upstairs Downstairs*. Bringing along cappuccino and espresso makers into the field, which had always seemed perfectly normal in the past, now had to done on the sly. One Trooper raised eyebrows from other GIs when, instead of pinning pornography centerfolds to the walls in his room, he hung vintage Vargas prints from the 1940s. When Executive Officer Lawrence Field told his fellow lieutenants to carry their riding crops as swagger sticks, they quickly shouted him down and made him swear to never breathe a word that he suggested the idea in the first place.

Playing hooky and other schoolboy escapades were executed with commando stealth. While undergoing further training in Hohenfels, Germany, a group of Troopers would leave the main gate each evening with bulging rucksacks each evening, acting as if they were going out for a long run. Their sergeant would see them leaving and think, "Wow, those guys must be really gung ho," not realizing that as soon as they reached the wood line, they would ditch their gear, change into civilian clothes, and hoof it to the village pub in local Schmidtmullen. The Troopers undergoing these jaunts thought of themselves as characters from *The Adventures of Tom Sawyer,* especially as they walked home through yellow rapeseed fields as the sun went down or when they stopped to swim in a local creek. In Bosnia, another group of guys would finagle riding sessions with the famous Lippizaner horses. Countless other such episodes took place on the sly, and are now lost to history.

*Stable Sergeant Richard Walkup rides a Lipizzaner. (Photo from Richard Walkup)*

By unanimous decision, the Troop's platoon sergeants vowed to never utter the word "Hooah," a morale-boosting yell used throughout the United States Army to demonstrate enthusiasm—real or imagined. Rejecting the use of "Hooah" struck a deep chord among Troopers who resisted lockstep mentalities within "Big Army" culture which seemed to insult a citizen-soldier's intelligence. This boycott led to some peculiar encounters.

One day, a regular army NCO concluded his training session with a robust "Hooah," expecting the requisite "Hooah" to echo back to him in return. But the entire platoon stared at him blankly in silence. The NCO, fearing that his own "Hooah" might have lacked sufficient enthusiasm, then gave his entire brief again and ended it with a more rousing "Hooah!" shout.

Again, however, the Troopers gave no response. Flummoxed, he repeated his entire speech for a yet third time, and ended with an especially loud, drawn out, "Hooooaaaahhhhh?" now posed as a question. But again, the thirty Troopers stared back at him while crickets chirped. Tom Farley, a Troop sergeant who had once been a cavalry officer, raised his hand and said, "Sergeant, sorry, but we don't 'Hooah' in this unit. From private to captain, not a single man here knows what you mean by it. Now you can go over to that tree and 'Hooah' it all you want, but we won't 'Hooah' back."

*The Troop in Bosnia, 2002. They'd snap to attention, but they wouldn't "Hooah!" (Photo from Thomas Boyle)*

Farley wasn't the only former officer to serve with the Troop in Bosnia as an NCO. Honorary Captain Keith Rogers—in a classic case of First City rank flip-flopping (harkening back to Robert Wharton in the War of 1812)—resigned his rank of major in order to deploy with the Troop to Bosnia as a staff sergeant. There he served as Captain Guenther's *driver*.

For years, it had been common practice for former officers to serve as Troop captains' drivers. For example, when Harry Gobora commanded the unit in the 1990s, he was ferried around by Sergeant Larry Swesey, a former major and West Point graduate who had led a cavalry platoon in Vietnam. Assuming a tutorial role, Swesey would gently intervene whenever Gobora was about to make a risky decision. As Gobora recalled, "Swesey would shake his head and say, 'I wouldn't do that if I were you, Sir.' And then I'd ask, 'Well what would you do if you *were* me—*Sergeant?*'" Swesey would reply by observing pros and cons about the scenario in question, based on his own army experience, and then let Captain Gobora draw his own conclusions.

Misunderstandings about Keith Rogers's rank created some comic run-ins with regular army officers. During a major readiness exercise, Rogers was manning the radios and looking after things in the TOC, as good NCOs do, when Lieutenant Hathaway came into the tent and asked him for an update on field situations. While Hathaway was still talking, Captain Guenther walked in with his regular army observer and asked for the same update. Hathaway replied, "Well, Keith just told me..." The regular army captain interrupted and said, "Keith? Who's Keith?" Hathaway said, "Oh sorry, Sir, I meant Sergeant Rogers here," gesturing with his hand. The visiting captain turned to Guenther and barked, "See, that's what I mean! Your officers can't be calling NCOs by their first names!" Hathaway agreed, "Sir, of course you're right! But back when I was an enlisted man, Sergeant Rogers here was our troop commander, so I still think of him as an officer." "Your *commander* in *this* Troop?" asked the confused visitor. When Hathaway, Rogers, and Gunther all nodded in confirmation, the gobsmacked visitor said nothing further on the topic.

## Chapter 29

# Putting Talents to Use

Upon arriving in Bosnia, Captain Guenther pondered his men's diverse talents and wondered how to use them. Some had Ivy League and even Oxbridge educations, others had foregone college completely, but in a symbiotic arrangement, the former held their more practical-minded brethren in high esteem while the latter kept a protective eye on the "brainiacs" who had trouble tying their own shoelaces. Considering this roster, Guenther thought, "How can the Troop best serve Bosnians during our limited stay, not as an occupying force, but as a recovery force?"

*(Previous page) Troop leaders during Bosnia train-up. (Photo from Thomas Boyle)*

Having researched the region with his wife, Guenther realized that the Troop had inherited what had once been the most highly contested part of Bosnia. While most other sectors were composed entirely of one ethnic group, Guenther's region had three: Croats, Bosniaks, and Serbs. He decided to assign each of his three platoons to specialize in one ethnic group. Describing the people in these three areas, Tom Farley said, "to my way of thinking, the Croatians were sort of like German Catholics, the Bosnians were Muslim, and the Serbs were Eastern Orthodox and essentially Russian." A ZOS (Zone of Separation) separated the Serb Republic from the Bosnian Federation. Much residual anger remained among the locals from decades of hard fighting.

Guenther and his lieutenants, who viewed the situation through the lens of their Wharton and University of Chicago MBAs, attributed this friction to market forces.

They figured that economic scarcity—as opposed to religious radicalism—was the root cause of the region's discord. They reckoned that a father unable to feed his family would turn to militant ethnic associations only as a last resort. This situation could be solved by job growth. To that end, Guenther decided to host meetings with local leaders to seek ways for them all to increase exports from local farms and factories. As laissez-faire businessmen, the Troop officers would field suggestions from their enlisted men for independent programs on an entrepreneurial basis.

Having survived the Tet Offensive in Vietnam, Farley was skeptical about Guenther's intention to treat the Bosnia deployment as an economic recovery mission. He assumed that the Bosnians hated each other for ancient reasons and didn't want any outside help. But after spending a few months in country, he changed his mind. "The Serbians and Croatians were lost," he said. "Their society was completely fractured, and they were certainly looking for outside help."

Jason Mayland, a University of Pennsylvania graduate whose Army rank was E4/ Specialist (ie, glorified Private), stepped forward with a cunning plan. Drawing on previous work with a Philadelphia city councilman, Mayland approached Gunther and said, "Sir, people like it when you do stuff for their kids. May I try to help local students prepare for SAT and ToEFL [Test of English as a Foreign Language] tests? Maybe we can use it to help them get into American schools." Guenther said, "OK, give it a try."

In order to get started, Mayland needed a Bosnian translator. But here he faced a roadblock, because translators were only assigned to officers. Although he was no officer, Mayland marched with considerable cheek into the Bosnian contractor's office hoping that the United States Army Specialist's rank insignia on his collar would remind the desk clerk of a Lieutenant's insignia in the German Army. This ploy worked, and Mayland was granted a personal translator for the rest of the year.

Aided by his interpreter, Mayland went to a local high school and assembled a group of gifted students who hoped to improve their English. Needing language tapes for each student, he took the cassettes in his possession, collected every tape recorder he could find on post, daisy-chained them together in the mess hall, recorded forty eight copies of language tapes all at once, and distributed them to his kids. He then selected course materials, made adequate photocopies, and lectured the students each week in a makeshift classroom. As he recalled, the classroom was very Spartan—illuminated by a bare light bulb hanging down from a string, with a broken slate chalkboard cracked along the top at a 45 angle. Eager to learn, the kids absorbed Mayland's teaching and performed very well, averaging combined math and language arts SAT scores of 1380 out of 1600.

While teaching the high school students, Mayland also created a college program. The idea for this occurred to him when he befriended an Austrian professor whom the United States Army had hired to teach cultural awareness to soldiers in Bosnia. The professor was bored at squadron headquarters, so Mayland invited him to set up a lecturing schedule at the Troop's base. Through a form of academic hocus pocus (akin to money laundering), Mayland arranged for Thomas Edison Teachers College in New Jersey to grant credits to these courses, which he then passed through the University of Maryland, whipping the whole shebang into a fully accredited college program. He then went door to door (using the summer-job sales tactics that helped put him through Penn) to sign up almost every Troop member. He enrolled eighty-nine people out of 101 men on post. As a result of Mayland's effort, the Troop logged the highest college participation rate of any unit in United States Army Europe.

Mayland wasn't the only person to treat Bosnia as an educational endeavor. Kevin Harper overcame his disappointment about not going to Afghanistan by treating his year in Bosnia as an academic sabbatical. Having studied chemistry and finance at Penn, he decided to round out his liberal arts education by listening to an audio program called

*The Great Courses*. Harper emailed the program's founder, Tom Collins, and explained that he was a soldier, and asked for some audio tapes. Collins responded by sending batches of freebies by mail. Harper listened to these while manning his 240B machine gun on Humvee patrols. In a twist of international First Troop networking, Harper later told Folef van Nispen, a Dutch Boyer Scholar, about the *Great Courses*. Nispen fell in love with the concept, and founded a Dutch version in the Netherlands called *Home Academy*, which is thriving today.

One of the Troop's main missions in Bosnia was "weapons harvesting"—gathering weapons and ammo from the local population, to prevent future armed conflicts. This procedure was easier said than done. Although many people wanted to get rid of the armaments left over from years of fighting, the Serbians had threatened to kill them if they didn't keep them hidden in stockpiles.

Guenther thought that preceding British occupation forces had exacerbated the problem by pushing too aggressively for disarmament: "The Brits would walk through town, carrying weapons at the high port, moving tactically in areas that called for a much softer approach, checking through ladies' underwear drawers for hidden guns. I would've expected us Yanks to go in like Rambo, not the Brits. But we did things in a very non-Rambo way." He subsequently learned that British soldiers took a harder line with Bosnians due to casualties they had sustained through long experience doing similar work in Northern Ireland.

After spending lot of time with little success, a few Troopers stumbled upon a possible solution. One day, a large shipment of Tootsie Rolls arrived from Wawa, a much-beloved

Philadelphia convenience store chain (owned by a family with historic Troop connections), that sent tons of free coffee and snack food to Philadelphia units in Bosnia. A number of soldiers picked through the Tootsie Rolls for a while, but the candy remained otherwise undisturbed for weeks. Noticing a misallocation of resources, a Trooper approached Captain Guenther and said, "Why not distribute these Tootsie Rolls to children on our patrols to see if it will help them get their parents to surrender more weapons to us?" This suggestion became a Troop program, jokingly called "Tootsie Roll Diplomacy."

In addition to diplomacy with Tootsie Rolls, Troopers tried other ways to improve civilian relations. Staff Sergeant George Anderson, a Valley Forge Military Academy professor and Citadel graduate, noticed that when he was briefed by the officer whose platoon Anderson's was about to replace, the briefing included photos and details of all the significant *locations* on site—the town hall, the police station, the local churches, and mosques—but made no mention of the most influential *townspeople*.

Anderson felt that success depended on knowing the right personalities, not the right buildings. So he devoted the next six months to learning about the people. As he discovered, "One man had just lost his wife of thirty years. Another wrote poetry. One of them especially liked chocolate. Another was threatening his neighbors." When Anderson's platoon left the region at the end of their tour, they presented their successors with a briefing book with 20% of its content devoted to locations and 80% to local people.

With time, the Bosnians started to surrender more and more weapons. Tom Farley said, "During the first weapons harvest, an old guy might bring out a Luger. But the second time around, he would sheepishly admit that he had a whole lot more stuff. Once we built a sufficient comfort level, the Bosnians started surrendering scores of weapons, munitions, and plastic explosives."

*Trooper Kevin Harper collects hand grenades during a weapons harvest. (Photo from Kevin Harper)*

One day, Sergeant William Wrabley, a lawyer and former United States Air Force officer, met a farmer who said, "I have some landmines you might want." For years, this man and his neighbors had been unearthing landmines while plowing their fields. The village stored all their collective landmines in this man's barn. The man stood about five feet two inches tall, and it was a good thing he wasn't an inch taller. Wrabley walked into the barn to behold a stack of landmines, fifty feet long, twenty feet deep, and six feet high—as high as the little man could reach. When the EOD (Explosive Ordinance Disposal) team arrived, they turned white, and explained that had the farmer been tall enough to stack those landmines one level higher, it would have produced enough pressure to detonate the entire bottom row!

*By deployment's end, the Troop assembled this handsome collection of weapons, which included a Thompson submachine gun, Russian sniper rifle, German MG 42 machine gun, Schmeiser submachine gun, and Russian submachine gun—all from World War II—and an AK-47 with a Shannon Dougherty Beverly Hills 90210 sticker lovingly placed on its stock. After filling out all the correct paperwork, they sent this cache home in a Conex box to the Troop's museum, but it never reached home. Some wags assert that a general may have wanted the contra ban for himself. (Photo from Richard Walkup)*

When the exhausted Troopers finally returned home from their deployment, they faced substantial financial setbacks from having been away from work for so long. Of course, they had all joined the unit understanding that financial sacrifice was a part of the Troop tradition dating back to its founding before the Revolutionary War. But many of them chose to leave the Active Roll to start new careers and salvage build old ones. Captain Lawrence Field kept the Troop alive on life support as its numbers briefly fell below required levels. When I asked Honorary Captain Tyler Hathaway to describe his return home, he shrugged and said, "Everyone came home proud to have been the first Troopers to serve overseas in fifty years, and to have accomplished their mission with no serious injuries."

# Chapter 30

# How I Joined the Troop

When the Troop returned from Bosnia in 2003, Elective Chairman David Thayer invited me by email to attend one of the unit's regular cocktail parties held on the third Thursday of each month. I eagerly took him up on the offer, and asked Andy White—my oldest childhood friend—to come along with me for moral support. Having grown up on a central Montgomery County fault line where the Philadelphia suburbs feathered into rural "Pennsyltucky," Andy and I were fascinated with exploring the hundreds of tiny volunteer organizations in the city. Having each done some traveling after college, Andy and I were starting to get the feeling that Philadelphia might be the most overlooked and under-rated city on earth.

Driving up to the Armory that night, we found the main gate open and inched the car through the portico and into the drill hall. A bunch of vehicles were already parked there, ranging in size, taste, and affluence. A large new BMW was parked next to a little Honda Civic, which sat next to a 1980s mint-condition Jaguar. Next to that was a beaten up Ford pickup truck. I parked next to the truck.

Inside the building, Andy and I heard a cacophony up in the NCO Club. Following the sound, we climbed a stairway to a large room filled with leather sofas, oriental rugs, and a sizeable crowd. The air was thick with cigar, pipe, and cigarette smoke.

To my acute discomfort, there was no way to quietly slip into the place undetected. As soon as we appeared at the top of the stairway, a number people noticed us instantly and extended hearty greetings. As MAMs (army slang for Military-Aged Males), we were immediately sized up as either threats or Troop prospects.

Suspicions were running high at that time, because the Troop's story had just been leaked to Hollywood! That's right; Adam Sandler's Happy Madison Film Company was working on a movie script called *The Fighting Quakers*. In the screenplay, a Philadelphia lawyer joins a fancy National Guard unit for business contacts, assured that the unit will never go to war. As soon as he enlists, the unit deploys to Bosnia, and chaos ensues.

Having just returned from Bosnia, Troopers speculated wildly about which of the unit's multiple lawyers had inspired Sandler. Considering Old Philadelphia's bipolar abhorrence of publicity ("Never get your name in the paper unless it's for your wedding or obituary") and penchant for theatrics, old hands shuddered at the thought of Hollywood making a film about America's oldest cavalry unit.

With so many cranks and eccentrics mixed in with so many others who were genuine pillars of the community, how could any movie ever get the tone exactly right? In such a climate, every Trooper was seen as a potential leak. And each new guest to the Armory was viewed as a possible spy.

As I looked around the room, I was impressed with how smartly many of the people were dressed. They wore blazers, tweeds, and camel-hair sport coats with neckties and even bowties (at a time when bowties weren't common outside

213

Philadelphia). Penny loafers and boat shoes without socks were very much in evidence—even though it was January. Indeed, the year was 2004, but the scene might have been torn from a page of the 1980 *Official Preppy Handbook*. I would eventually learn that it's the rare Trooper who doesn't care about clothes.

After mixing around the room for a bit, someone introduced us to Andy Sullivan, Chairman of the Elective Committee, who sat perched at the bar on a stool, wearing a blazer, Troop necktie, and what I perceived at the time to be an arrogant smirk.

Just as we approached, a Trooper behind the bar placed a fresh martini down gently in front of him. Ignoring his drink, Sullivan engaged us in some introductory chitchat: "So, how'd you hear about us?" he inquired. We gave our stories. He listened a bit and then launched into an interrogation, seeking to peg our social origins. Although I had experienced that sort of social sniffing to some extent back in England, I was surprised to see it take such a Dickensian form here in Pennsylvania. Among other strategic things, he asked "where had we gone to school?" Were we "from the area" (i.e., did we have ancestors who fought in the Revolution)? Were we "involved with any other clubs in town?" Did we have any experience riding horses? Then he asked, "Do you realize this is an army unit, and not just a club?" Rattled, we responded to each question most uneasily, fearing that nothing we said would be right. Having raked us over the coals for a while, Sullivan remembered his martini, the contents of which were still bulging over the rim of its glass on the bar. He picked it up gingerly, took a dainty sip, and then his face contorted in mock pain. At the bartender, he screamed, "You call this a *martini!?*" and then he tossed the contents of his drink on the floor at our feet, soaking the carpet. Then he bawled to the bartended, "Make me another!" and swiveled his bar chair back toward us in one single motion.

Appalled at this behavior, we were about to leave. But then to our surprise, his toned suddenly softened. He laughed at himself, smiled warmly and said, "Welcome to the Armory! Stay as long as you want! Come back anytime! If you want to learn more about the First City Troop, come to our next monthly dinner." Then he pointed to his eyes with two fingers, waved us off and said, "I'll be keeping my eye on you!"

I later found out that Sullivan's abrasive treatment had all been an act. Because members of the Troop are forced to spend so much time with each other on drill weekends and annual training, they liked to test newcomers to discover their motives. Although Sullivan seemed pretentious that first night, I soon discovered that he was quite down-to-earth and that he abhorred behavior that smacked of putting on airs.

The most memorable person I met that first night at the Armory was Crawford Pennypacker (not his real name, but naturally, the name he chose for this book). He was in his early twenties, tallish, boyish looking, and very clean-cut in a way that reminded me of American college students just before the Vietnam War. Pennypacker had fascinating parentage. His dad had grown up rich on the Philadelphia Main Line and traced his ancestors to the Mayflower. His mother was a first-generation American, with parents straight from Ireland. Brought up by parents of such divergent social backgrounds, Pennypacker prided himself in the ability to mix with anyone, a trait intentionally cultivated by many Troopers. Thoroughly charming, he could be volatile at times. His old-world upbringing had given him little preparation for the modern world. When I met him, he was earning his living by "faux painting"—that is, daubing the walls and floors of old houses with brush strokes to make them look like they were made of marble or mahogany. Although this practice was common enough in 18th-century America (George Washington's house at Mount Vernon featured quite a bit of it), it was quite rare in 2005!

Up to that point in time, life had taught me that I tend to be happiest when surrounded by strong and eccentric characters. The Troop certainly seemed like a goldmine in this regard. So, I eagerly followed Sullivan's advice to attend more of their events. Tom Farley offered to be my sponsor during this process. For his opening line he said "I guess the first thing you need to know is that we're just one, big—exceedingly dysfunctional—family."

On Armory visits, it was fascinating to glance at the bulletin board where press clippings of Troopers were posted. These could be wildly divergent. Last summer for example, an article about a deceased Trooper whose 18th-century Chester County farm had just gone into a land trust was tacked beside an article about a former Trooper whose estranged wife had shot him with an heirloom derringer. Leave it to a Trooper to get shot by an antique pistol.

A long election process now stretched before me. The first step was to get a sponsor, someone already in the unit, who would submit a form stating that I wanted to stand for a "First Reading" to the "Active Roll." This reading would be a statement of intent. My next step after that would be to enlist straight into the Pennsylvania National Guard as a United States Army private. If the army accepted me, I could stand for a "Second Election" to the Active Roll at the next Troop dinner.

If I made it through that, I could then be a Trooper. As you can see, one has to join the National Guard before joining the Troop, which requires quite the leap of faith.

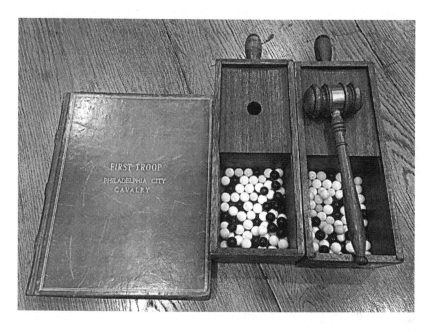

*The ancient register, gavel, and boxes with black and white marbles used for electing new members into the Troop. When standing for his "Second Election to the Active Roll," a candidate must wait in the NCO Club downstairs while the wooden boxes are passed around the mess hall for a vote. White and black marbles mean "yes" and "no" respectively. Nowadays, it is very rare for a candidate to get blackballed, unless they are intentionally refuse to act like gentlemen. In past generations, personality clashes and hidden social factors clashes made Troop election a much thornier to process. (Author's photo)*

In order to navigate the election process, I considered some things my dad had taught me. With his deep family roots

217

in the rural Philadelphia area, he lectured me as a kid to be low-key when dealing with people socially. He preached the opposite of "chutzpah," stressing the need to avoid being pushy and to not boast about oneself. His dad had often used the term "quiet elegance" to describe how a person's manners, clothes, and external style should all line up with his internal character. These aesthetic and moral aspects of taste pervaded everything in life, from furniture to cars to houses to one's choice of friends. The main idea was that if you have good traits, the right people will notice them over time—even if it takes *years*. Eventually they will notice that you are holding certain things back, and they will respect you all the more for it. However, if you try throwing your weight around, those same people will write you off without your ever knowing it.

Although such understated behavior might get you eaten alive in New York City, it was woven deep into the Delaware Valley cultural fabric, and I noticed that it applied in England and Germany as well. I figured that if I stood around the more established Troopers like a piece of furniture for long enough, good things might happen. It was hard to have the kind of patience my dad preached, but I had faith in what you might call the Philadelphia social-maturation rate. In the final reckoning, Philadelphia is not exclusive toward new faces, but it is certainly *slow*.

Naturally, people who either don't understand or who reject Philadelphia's unwritten rules join the Troop all the time. Some have approached the Troop assuming that they could blow out the cobwebs, put their stamp on things, run the show, and save the culture from itself. But that approach only seems to work if applied at a glacial pace. Otherwise, it's easy to shipwreck on the invisible shoals of other egos.

After I had attended a few Troop events, Honorary Captain Guenther took me to lunch at the Merion Cricket Club for a friendly opening chat. In that gracious setting, he described the Troop as an "open elite" that constantly seeks new blood and talent. He said, "Before Bosnia, people often mocked us for 'dressing up to play army' while staying safe in Pennsylvania. After hearing snide comments like that for long enough, we even started to believe it ourselves. Bosnia was hard on everyone but great for the Troop, because it proved we are legitimate citizen-soldiers."

Guenther closed by stressing that there is *never* a convenient time to join the Troop. He warned, "If you feel called to join us, then go ahead and do it. If you put it off, you may lose your window of opportunity. There are guys my age and older who didn't join the Troop when they had the chance, and they resent us today because they wished they had served." With such counsel, what could I do? I decided to take the plunge.

At 04:30 a.m. (the normal start time for most things military), Staff Sergeant Lee Page, the A-Troop's full-time National Guard recruiter, picked me up at the Armory to drive me to the Military Entrance Processing Station (MEPS) at Fort Dix, New Jersey.

Going through MEPS is a First Troop rite of passage. In a way, it's the most intimidating step of all because it's where you sign up for a six-year commitment to the United States Army. Kevin Harper described it as "the creepiest moment in my military career, the first time in my life I was ever treated like an automaton and a piece of meat!" Like many Troopers, he compared it to the opening scene of the prison film *Shawshank Redemption*. (For my generation, that movie often seemed to capture nuances of military life more than any war film ever did.)

With a rag-tag group of strangers, most of them straight out of high school, I was herded through a battery of medical and aptitude tests. Like nervous people anywhere, some of my new companions were very quiet and others chattered away endlessly—a dynamic which would prove to be an army constant.

One guy memorably bragged that he could tell what brand of cigarettes a person smoked just by looking at him. Doubting him, I said, "Dude, you're full of shit!" "No man," he insisted, "I really can!" So I challenged him and asked, "OK, then what kind of cigarettes do I smoke? That is, if I even smoke at all." (This was a trick question. I did smoke cigarettes, but no one ever thought I looked like a guy who would smoke. My favorite brand, if I were forced to choose one, would have been Camel Lights.) Accepting my challenge, he took a long glance at me and then said, *"Camel Lights!"* The army is full of people like that who are savants in assessing human nature.

All day, everyone snickered about a rumor that in the final physical inspection, the doctor would make everyone drop his trousers and stand against the wall so he could check for anal abnormalities. Toward the end of the day, we were led into a medical room where, sure enough, that event occurred. Feeling thus violated, we were then ushered into a room for swearing in. Those of us joining the Pennsylvania National Guard swore an oath of allegiance to our state governor. Those entering the regular military swore an oath to the President of the United States.

Having irrevocably enlisted into the National Guard, I attended the next monthly Troop meeting to stand for my Second Reading to the Active Roll. My stomach—as might well be imagined—was in knots.

It was a typical monthly dinner, held on the first Monday night of the month. Everyone wore coats and ties. Fines were imposed on anyone improperly dressed. Prime rib was served with boiled potatoes and vegetables. Beer and wine flowed freely, the consumption of which lubricated the business proceedings in 2005 just as they had since colonial times.

(When the First City Troop held a farewell party for George Washington in 1787 at City Tavern, fifty five gentlemen consumed fifty four bottles of Madeira, sixty bottles of claret, eight bottles of old stock, twenty two bottles of porter, eight bottles of cider, and twelve bottles of beer. They also stood drinks for the event's musicians. There was also the cost of broken wine glasses, decanters, and tumblers. Washington's farewell partly cost about $16,000 in today's money.)

Throughout dinner, people called on each other to sing Troop songs. Anyone called had to stand on his chair and belt out one of the many songs accumulated over the years. I noticed that whenever one of the more polished Troopers stood up to speak, he would button his coat in a senatorial fashion, say what he had to say, and then unbutton his coat in one smooth motion as he sat back down. "Very civilized touch," I thought. This elegant custom was equally followed whether a man rose to elaborate a fine point in debate, or to sing a bawdy song like *Charlotte the Harlot.*

After eating, I was shown downstairs to the NCO Club with other guests to wait while members above voted on new elections. There was one other prospective Trooper with me that night: Carlton, an Air Force Academy graduate with a genteel Kentucky accent who was working for Senator Arlen Spector. He seemed so mature and accomplished. Compared with him, I felt like chopped liver.

Someone finally came down and led us up to the main stairs mess hall. The doors were closed, and we were told to wait until the election results were tallied. My stomach was busy performing its now full-time job of tying itself into knots. The door finally opened. I stood up, but Carlton was ushered in, and the door then shut behind him, almost in my face. In the mess hall I could hear rowdy shouts of applause, followed by everyone loudly singing a Troop song.

Things settled down a bit. Then the door opened again. It was my turn now. Did I make it? I entered the room to thunderous applause. "Thank God," I thought. Relieved but embarrassed at the clapping, I stared at the floor as someone led me to the head table. Someone hissed, "Face the captain and salute!" I obediently turned and saluted Captain Lawrence Field. He saluted back, then leaned across the table, grabbed my lapel, and pinned a First City Troop rosette to the buttonhole.

Huzzah, my Troop Rosette!

*A rosette (above) is a little flower-like pin that Philadelphia men wear on their coat lapels to indicate club memberships. To my knowledge, the only firm that produces them in America is Dexter Rosettes, located just outside the city. The Troop rosette's colors are an untrendy brown, buff, and gold—the exact same colors the Gloucester Hunt Club adopted in 1766. By tradition, Troopers wear this pin with every suit, sport coat, and blazer (as shown in the photograph below). They may not wear any other rosette, even if they belong to other organizations that have them. Modern Troopers have even worn rosettes on their body armor in Iraq! (Photo from Dexter Rosettes, Inc. and First City Troop collection)*

As I signed my name into the Troop's roll book, I was assigned an official number, 2383, which indicated that I was the 2,383rd man to join the unit since 1774. From that moment on, I would be expected to sign letters and emails to other members with the following archaic 18th-century closing:

"Your Most Obedient Servant,

Drew Meschter 2383."

# Chapter 31

# "Basic Hazing"

Joining the Troop might have thrown a wrench into my career plans—had I had any. But I joined at a time when everything in life was in flux. Having just returned from Heidelberg, I was unemployed, living with my parents, and feeling like a ne'er-do-well. I hoped to get basic training out of the way before settling into harness with a grown-up career.

As a Trooper, I could pick one of the following three military jobs: armor (driving a tank), mortars (a form of infantry-artillery), or scouting (observing and reporting). I chose "19D" as a Military Occupational Specialty (MOS)— Cavalry Scout. "Cav" scouts operate beyond front lines, seeking to engage enemy forces without being detected, while communicating their movements back to higher command. If scouts face weaker enemies, they destroy them; if they discover superior forces, they hide or escape from them. This role's yin-yang balance attracted me greatly.

Each military MOS has its own subculture. Civilians familiar with Hollywood portrayals of gung-ho marines, suave naval aviators, and intrepid special forces would be surprised to discover the esprit cultivated in less dashing MOSs like truck driving, accounting, and laundry. American cavalry scouts have their own sense of self, with cultural roots stretching back to the Civil War and earlier. Scouts wear Stetson hats and spurs with their dress uniforms. They operate in small groups, cultivate a freewheeling approach to things, and celebrate a bias for improvisation on the fly. In the bureaucratic world of "Big Army," scouts are sort of romantic.

In *Boots on the Ground*, a first-hand account of the 2003 Iraq invasion, Karl Zinsmeister described cavalrymen's personalities "as slashing and devil-may-care." Comparing scouts to other soldiers like helicopter pilots and airborne infantry, he said, "For cavalry troopers, it's almost impossible to re-create within a training exercise the free-floating, slash-and-burn buccaneering that combat brings." There aren't many scouting units in the United States Army, so 19Ds are what you might call a "boutique" specialty.

As I counted the weeks until basic training, Andy Sullivan (the man who tossed his martini on the floor during that first visit to the NCO Club) invited me to join him and a bunch of other Troopers to attend the National Debutante Cotillion in Washington, D.C. The "D.C. Deb Ball," as we called it, was an annual coming-out party for young ladies, most of them Southern. Cadets and Midshipmen from West Point and Annapolis would escort them in their full-dress uniforms with great pageantry, with a few First City Troopers sprinkled in as well, on occasion. Things were tense at those events in the early 2000s because many of the graduating soldiers, sailors, and marines were heading straight for Afghanistan or Iraq.

At the ball that year, I fell smitten for a fascinating Virginia girl. She was a proper horsewoman: jocular and tomboyish enough to be a buddy, but brought up to be a gracious southern lady. She seemed to think of herself as the modern incarnation of a 1930s sportswoman along the lines of Katherine Hepburn. Or maybe that's just how I saw her. Crawford Pennypacker was there the night we met. He dozed on the sofa in the Troop's Hilton hotel suite while she and I chatted and joked around until dawn. Occasionally, he'd wake up, pick grapes from a bowl next to his head, toss them at our faces, and then fall back to sleep. She said it was noble that I was about to ship off to Fort Knox for basic training and that Pennypacker was deploying to Iraq. I was thrilled to find a girl who might become my pen pal during the coming ordeal.

Eager for information about what basic training would be like, I pumped lots of Troopers for stories about their own Fort Knox experiences. Many of their tales were laugh-out-loud funny. Some may have even been based on actual fact.

Here's one of the more doubtful stories that old-hands insist to be true: Sometime in the 1950s, Troopers John Biddle and David Swope were standing next to each other at cavalry school when a limousine pulled up. Nodding to the chauffer, Biddle tossed his M1 rifle to Swope, said, "Hold this for a minute," hopped into the car, and was whisked away. A few days later, he returned much refreshed from a weekend at Martha's Vineyard. I guess in the old days anything was possible.

There's an old joke that new members are treated kindly when the join the Troop, because the army takes care of our hazing. "Ha ha ha, yep, the First City Troop is the only fraternity in the U.S. that outsources its hazing to the federal government!" The rub lays not so much in the rigors of training, but from the countless opportunities for the average Trooper to feel like a fish out of water in Army life.

For extra laughs, older Troopers often try to engineer situations that exacerbate this fish-out-of-water effect. In 1985, for example, the night before James Hanlon and Jonathan Duffy departed for basic training, their sponsor, Law Fotterall, invited them to a big send-off dinner. Big-brother like, he earnestly explained, "Now guys, when you get Fort Knox, they'll take away your civilian clothes within hours of your arrival. That brief time window is your one chance to make a lasting impression on the drill sergeants. To start things off on the right foot, make sure you wear blazers, pressed chinos, polished loafers, and Troop neckties. And while you're at it, you should probably wear Troop crests on those blazers as well." Hanlon and Duffy heartily thanked Fotterall for his expert advice. Thus attired, they departed for Kentucky like lambs to the slaughter, and stepped off the bus at Fort Knox to face a jeering crowd of new best friends in tattoos, muscle shirts, and cutoff jeans.

With these anecdotes fresh in mind, I began my rite of passage in January 2005 with two other Troopers, Wilson Ryans (not his real name) and John Faller. From what I heard later, the minute we left the Armory for Fort Knox, a bunch of guys in the NCO Club started placing bets on how each of us would fare.

As fish out of water, each of us foundered differently. Faller, a rough-hewn Texan who joined the Troop because it seemed like the closest modern equivalent to being in the Civil War horse cavalry, was well prepared for army life, so he swam like a marlin. That guy was a fish *in* water. Ryans, an effete Michigander who discovered the Troop while working in Philadelphia after college, was utterly impervious to military mannerisms. He attracted drill sergeants' ire like a lightning rod. Although it's hard to be objective about my own performance in retrospect, I was pretty effete myself, and I tended to drift mentally off into space like an absent-minded professor.

The professor act was sometimes affected but sometimes genuine. I embraced Fort Knox as an educational exercise, as if it were a college elective—*Soldiering 101.* I saw it as a chance to build character and to become a citizen-soldier in the Athenian tradition. More than anything, I saw it as the final step needed to round out my liberal arts education. For many Troopers, the chance to build new social skills by mixing with people from different backgrounds is the opportunity of a lifetime—no less important than graduating from a good prep school or college.

It all began with Reception. Everyone remembers *that* jarring experience. We arrived late at night by bus, got yelled at and herded around through various processing stations. They shaved our heads, issued us running shorts and sweat suits (we weren't worthy of uniforms yet), hustled us through piles of paperwork, assigned us to a prison-like barracks—a guy next to me actually said "this reminds me of when I was in jail!"—fed us chow, and forced us to stand outside for long stretched of time doing roll call in the freezing cold.

In one room, a drill sergeant told us we could ditch any contraband items on our persons, such as tobacco, pornography, weapons, and drugs into an "amnesty box," with no questions asked. One Trooper who was there in the 1980s didn't have anything to drop into the box, but—with astounding cheek—reached his hand *into* the box to see what he might find. His fingertips fell on two marijuana joints, which he pulled out, stuffed into his briefs, and squirreled away for safe keeping. Three months later, he and a fellow Trooper were huddled under their shelter-halves in a driving rain, lying in the mud as water dripped into their ears. The other Trooper was especially miserable because the next day was his birthday. At the stroke of midnight, he tapped his comrade awake, produced the two joints and said "Happy birthday, buddy!" They each lit up and smoked together, turning what might have been one of life's lowest points into a brilliant memory (and tribal legend).

Basic training is highly theatrical, choreographed with the aim of breaking each man out of his civilian identity and building him back up again as a soldier and member of a team. Drill sergeants used the word "individual" as an epithet. The Army had recently changed its TV advertising slogan from the challenging *Be All That You Can Be* to the self-indulgent *Army of One.* This new slogan was meant to make people feel "special," and to extol their sense of individuality, but the drill turned it into an insult. Pointing to a private, one drill sergeant might say, "Would you look at that joker? Fucker thinks he's an *individual.*" His fellow drill sergeant would answer back, "That's right, Battle [battle buddy], he's an *Army of One.*"

The Battle Buddy concept was big at basic training. It was meant to teach everyone to look out for each other. Each of us had to have a "battle buddy"—a fellow soldier—with him at all times, even when doing private things like going to the latrine. As one chaplain explained, "Ecclesiastes says two are better than one. If one man falls down, the other can help him up. One man might be overpowered, but two can defend themselves." Woe to the recruit spotted without a battle buddy! If a single private was caught walking around on his own, his whole squad or platoon might get "smoked" by the drill sergeants.

Getting "smoked" was army slang for intense physical exercise used as punishment. From the first day at Fort Knox, we dreaded smoke sessions, but eventually got accustomed to them. Drill sergeants knew a whole range of anaerobic exercises that could inflict pain through the handy means of lactic acid. Although these smoke sessions were trying, the drill sergeants' dialogue surrounding them was often *hilarious*.

For example, a drill sergeant says "Private, why don't you get down and do some push-ups." The private drops down, does two or three push-ups, and asks "Permission to recover, Drill Sergeant?" In mock astonishment, the Drill Sergeant exclaims "What the fuck, Private!" The wise-ass private plaintively responds, "You said do *some* push-ups, Drill Sergeant," so the drill sergeant explodes, "Why you smug little shit. You're gonna stay down there and push until your feeble fucking arms shove the Earth off of its axis and send us spiraling off into the sun!"

One soldier recalled a recruit whose thick dark hair had a widow's peak evident which remained evident even with his head shaved. A drill sergeant thought that private looked like the Count from Sesame Street. So whenever he got smoked, he had to do a Count impersonation, shouting out the numbers "One, ah-ah-ah, two, ah-ah-ah, three, ah-ha-ha..." for each pushup.

Drill sergeants used the army's water-drinking policy as a weapon against our bladders. There once was a time, back in World War II, when trainees were only allowed to drink minimal amounts of water in field exercises, in order to develop "water discipline." Israeli research later discovered that soldiers operate substantially better when fully hydrated, not when running on empty, and the U.S. military followed suit with the zeal of the converted. Our generation was therefore trained from day one that "hydration" was paramount. The drill sergeants said "Privates, try to drink enough water so that

231

when you piss, it's clear. If it looks like lemonade, you're OK. If it looks like apple juice, you're in trouble."

Knowing that we were constantly gorged with water, and that we had to sit around for hours in classroom training, the drill sergeants used latrine breaks as a way to torture us— and as a way to build self-discipline and group cooperation. When standing in formation or sitting in class, no single person was permitted to go to the bathroom unless everyone was dismissed at once as a group. Whenever the drill sergeants would periodically release us for breaks, a hundred guys would run and jostle to queue up for two porta-johns in the parking lot outside. Before half the group got through using the latrines, the drill sergeants would start counting down until we all got back into the building. During the first week, half the group would have to get back into the building before they could relieve themselves. We quickly learned to treat these potty breaks with all dispatch. Through external peer-pressure and internal bladder/intestinal pressure, our company learned to hustle everyone through the facilities with lighting efficiency.

The urination problem may be an ancient one for soldiers in all armies. There's an adage that when a man once asked General George Patton for the best advice he could give to a soldier for life in the military, he said "Piss when you can."

With no beer, cigarettes, books (except for religious books like the Bible), magazines, internet, television, telephone, or music, I suffered withdrawal from civilian amusements on multiple levels. Having no access to music, I was surprised to find that bubble-gummy British pop songs would cycle through my head on a constant basis, perhaps because their cheerful tones were so antithetical to our harsh conditions. At morning formation, Duran Duran and Petula Clark were constant companions.

Faced with the all the privations and pressures scientifically designed into basic training, some recruits crumbled. The army knew this would happen, so the drill sergeants took suicide threats very seriously. Trooper Austin Lamac recalled that when he was at Fort Knox, a private told his battle buddy that he wanted to himself. In a trice, he was whisked onto "suicide watch": he had to sit in a room for 24 hours while his peers took shift watching him "in line of sight" to prevent him from harming himself. Eventually he came to terms with things and finished basic training with everyone else.

It quickly dawned on me that basic training is very, very, very *basic*. Some of the things we had to learn were quite complicated, but the learning process was broken down into its simplest individual parts, so that anyone could learn them. From a 30,000 foot view, the system is pure genius; from the 1-foot view it can be mind-numbing.

The mindless aspects of military routine had a penitential effect on me. Its alien environment forced me to reflect on life in ways that I never had before, to wonder if I had made the right decisions over the years. The Anglican confession would often spring to mind from Durham Cathedral:

> "Most merciful God, we confess that we have sinned against you in thought and word and deed, through negligence, through weakness, through our own deliberate fault."

At these times, I would find myself ruminating about how I might have wronged people in the past, and would meditate on ways to learn from those mistakes, or make amends.

This phenomenon is something that many Troopers experience, and which knits us together as brothers. We flounder as privates in the army, until military culture teaches us new things that college could never have taught. And much of what we learn would be lost on preppy friends back home.

Andrew Leighton wanted to become a Marine Corps officer after graduating from Georgetown University. He took the PT test, scored just a notch below perfect, and was told to come back to try again sometime. He discovered the Troop, and embraced it as a more interesting alternative. Reflecting on his dark moments at basic training, he said, "One of the biggest things that encouraged me was that I knew I was doing this for a purpose outside of the Army, and I knew who and what I was going back to. I wasn't going to be shipped off to Alaska or Louisiana, like everyone else, to live the Army life. I was here for some training and then I was going back to be a Trooper."

The drill sergeants made a big deal about "Dear John" letters, warning us that the girls we left behind were bound to stray. This ancient army melodrama was rife with terminology and folklore. "Jody" was the catch-all name for any cad "back on the block" (at home) who might try to make a move on "Susie" or "Sally," the girl who belonged to "Joe" (the catch-all name for any American soldier). The drills knew from bitter experience that many privates would get dumped, and that some would end up on suicide watch as a result. Periodic explosions broke out in my own platoon, when some of the younger guys got these dreaded break-up letters. For many of them, it was their first time away from home. They clung to the

234

fiction—held by many college freshmen—that high-school romances will last beyond first semester. Instead of soft-pedaling this, the drill sergeants rubbed it in, hoping to give victims the chance to steel themselves in advance.

"How many of you privates have girlfriends back home who just loooooved to fuck?" cried one drill sergeant to his unsuspecting platoon. A bunch of lusty privates howled back "Hooooaaaahhhhh," in the affirmative. After a dramatic pause, the drill sergeant said, "Well guess what, privates? *They still do!*"

All this "Jody" stuff sent my thoughts drifting back to the Virginia girl from the D.C. Deb Ball. She wasn't my girlfriend by any means, but she had become a treasured pen pal. She was living in New York City by that point—a place with many, many options for unattached women. Although I couldn't have been a priority for her, she was kind enough to send periodic notes on personal stationery, spritzed with perfume and spiced with witty innuendo (appropriate for a 1930s sportswoman). At mail call each night, I'd stand at parade-rest with stomach aflutter as the drill sergeant sorted through the incoming post. He would pick each letter out of the bag one by one, call out a name, and then fling the envelope down the hall at the recipient's face with amazing accuracy.

Although loneliness kept the D.C. girl in mind as a constant apparition, the hilarity of life in an all-male combat training platoon helped compensate immensely.

Having attended co-ed schools all my life, and having grown up with sisters, I welcomed the chance to spend a few months away from female influence. It was sort of like a science experiment. Back in high school, a friend once said,

"Drew, your personality would be totally different if you had brothers." I didn't know what he meant at the time, but life at Fort Knox clarified his comment. When guys don't have females to counterbalance them, they live a much simpler and more direct form of existence. They challenge each other constantly, and hold each other to baser, more block-headed standards. As iron sharpens iron, one man sharpens another. Male environments breed stoicism, insensitivity, and even abuse, but they are amazingly light-hearted. Humor is the main form of social currency. It melts all barriers. Anything is fair game for a confrontation or a joke. This dynamic has to be experienced to be understood, and it may explain why I've never met a male who didn't grieve when his boarding school, club, or military unit became coed. I think society loses something when guys lose the chance to challenge and develop each other as guys.

It often occurred to me that humor is magnified by hierarchy. By that, I mean that when someone in authority makes a joke, it tends to seem funnier than if someone on your level said it—perhaps because it breaks the tension of command. Also, I realized that humor is highly dependent on rules and situational norms. The more rules and norms you have in a given social environment, the more chances you get to break them and screw things up.

With all its unwritten assumptions about adolescent masculine behavior and its by-the-book adherence to standard operating procedure, each day in army life was a gag reel waiting to happen. And the drill sergeants knew how to spout jokes, diatribes, and witty asides at just the right moment for comedic effect. They'd often use comical call-and-response commands, shouting things out that required a pre-scripted response. For example, in order to get his men to drink enough water, a drill sergeant might assemble his men and shout "Platoon, prepare to drink." Everyone in the platoon would have to whip out his canteen and open the cap with lighting speed. Then he would shout, "Drink! Water!" to which the privates had to respond, "Beat the heat, Drill Sergeant! Beat the heat!" They'd have to down their canteens at once, and then hold them upside down over the heads with the cap off to prove they were empty.

Like a family with too many kids, we squabbled constantly and were lightning quick to learn Army insults, such as Shit Bag (a lazy person who tries to hid and shirk duties) and Blue Falcon (a play on the acronym BF, which stands for Buddy Fucker—a guy who betrays his comrades.) The moment we learned these expressions, everyone started using them on each other. Any private who tried to boss his peers around was called a Drill Private. A private quick to memorize rules and regulations, and then counsel his peers with superior knowledge was called a Barracks Lawyer.

Anything the drill sergeants told us to do triggered instant competition to do it first and best. By degrees, I lapsed into a juvenile sharp-elbowed "me-first" attitude that eroded years of cultivation. After ten minutes of dealing with me after Fort Knox, my sister—appalled at my new manners—said, "You were so polite when you came home from Heidelberg, and now you're worse than you were in junior high school!"

Setting up tents was always a *fiasco*. The Army's GP Medium (General Purpose Medium) tent was large enough to sleep a twelve-man squad and heavy/ complicated enough to require much team work in setting up. Our drill sergeants demonstrated how to set the tent up once or twice and then let us figure it out from then on. Left to ourselves, chaos reigned. Each private wanted to be the head honcho, to tell everyone else how to stretch the tent out on the ground, drive the stakes in, and raise the poles. It became a huge ego thing. With everyone trying to tell everyone else what to do, any one person who tried to be boss would get ignored by the others. (This phenomenon occurred to me in retrospect when I read the following passage in Alexis de Tocqueville's *Democracy in America*: "A man in democratic times is extremely reluctant to obey his neighbor, who is his equal. He refuses to recognize in his neighbor enlightenment superior to his own... He likes to make his neighbor constantly aware of the fact that both are dependent on the same master." Normal American soldiers certainly bear out Tocqueville's 19th-centry observations today—especially when they are First City Troopers.)

Well into training, however, the tent thing sort of worked itself out. Everyone in my platoon reached a tacit agreement of shared responsibility. At first, certain guys took ownership of certain parts of the process, some of them gravitating toward the guy lines, others to the tent poles, and others to the stakes. As this system of proprietorship took root, GP Medium tent pitching became easy. Years later, I discovered that Soviet Army used to use tent pitching as one of their primary methods for determining leadership potential in new recruits.

Meal times at the chow hall were crowning high points each day—the only chance to indulge. But even these moments were designed to pass too quickly for comfort. Each man was allowed five minutes to eat once he sat down. If anyone seemed to be relaxing over his meal, a drill sergeant might walk up and say, "OK, you're all done eating," and everyone at the table would have to stand up mid-bite and leave the chow hall. Having been an annoyingly slow eater all my life before joining the army, I quickly I learned to inhale my food by arranging the things on my tray into an assembly line.

Meal times in the field were sociologically fascinating. In the field, we each got a Meal Ready to Eat (MRE), the standard U.S. military field ration. After pushing and shoving to receive our MREs from a drill sergeant—who would keep us from choosing our favorite meals based on the label—we would sit on the ground Indian style, circling around first like dogs to find the best spots, and then eating in buddy groups of three or four. Thirty of us would sit within shouting distance. As each man tore into his MRE package, a free-slowing auction would occur as everyone tried to trade preferred food items. It was like the barter economy you hear about in prisons where cigarettes act as currency. Within weeks, each person mastered amazing market knowledge, memorizing the food tastes of everyone else in the platoon, and applying that knowledge to gain bargaining leverage.

For example, if I liked peanut butter more than Skittles, and Skittles were in more demand than peanut butter, I could leverage Skittles (whenever I got them) for double amounts of peanut butter. But someone would soon notice my tendency, blurt it out to the rest of the group, and ruin my bargaining power. So you learned to fake things sometimes and bargain for food you didn't like, to create a smokescreen. Certain food items *zero* bargaining value, such as the bread which tasted like cardboard. If someone got stuck with bread and tried to trade it off, he would get laughed at.

With our voracious appetites, it was hard for the overweight guys (called "fat bodies") to lose weight. It was fascinating to watch how the fat guys finally lost weight. The calisthenics and running we did each morning never seemed to make a dent in them. But once we started marching to and from our training areas each day—just one mile out and one mile back, before and after lunch—their fat melted away. The frequent walking must have triggered their metabolism more than running. Soon they slimmed down and their uniforms hung on them like clown suits.

Speaking of uniforms, it was exciting to get issued our uniforms, weapons, and equipment. Going through lines while supply ladies dumped countless items into our duffel bags felt like Christmas. After we got all our stuff, the drill sergeants made us dump our duffle bag contents on the floor. Then they explained what each thing was and how it worked. They explained all this with fascinating attention to detail.

For example, we were each issued two pairs of boots. So Drill Sergeant Oxendine sat us all down to explain how they worked. "How boots work?" you ask. Yes. He showed us how to smooth our socks over our feet before putting the boots on. He explained how the insoles worked, how to lace one pair of boots with a knot at the bottom, and the other without a knot at the bottom so we could tell the two pairs apart. He told us to alternate wearing them each day, to give each pair a day off to dry out and breathe. Then he took us into the laundry room and showed us how to brush them off in the sink under running water, before adding a new layer of black polish each night. After all this, he concluded, "OK, Privates, now you know how to take care of your boots. You've all seen me do it, and I'm not going to show you again. Got it?" "Yes, Drill Sergeant!" we shouted.

Next, he did the same thing with our uniforms, demonstrating how to wear the trousers up on the natural waist line, how to fasten the buttons on every pocket, and how to don and doff the hat. "Privates, the instant your foot touches the threshold as you walk into a building, you remove your cover (hat). The second your boot hits the threshold leaving a building, you put it back on. Got it?!" By showing us in such detail how to "operate" boots and uniforms, the drill sergeants set a standard for how we would later care for our weapons, vehicles, and each other.

All this painstaking instruction triggered a new urge to apply a diligence-in-the-small-things mentality to all areas of life. Years later, I read that John Wooden—one of the most successful collegiate basketball coaches ever—took the same approach as our drill sergeants. He would begin each playing season by teaching his new boys how to put their shoes and socks on properly, reasoning that excellence in that one basic area would lay the groundwork for future success in everything else. (The devout Wooden may have taken his cue from Jesus, who said "Whoever can be trusted with very little can also be trusted with much.")

Diligence aside, much of the training we received at Fort Knox washed over me like a blur. The hours seemed to pass slowly, but the days slipped by quickly. Our daily routine was as follows:

04:30 Wake up/personal hygiene

05:00 Formation for accountability

05:15 Physical training

06:10 Breakfast

06:30 Change into uniform

06:45 Formation for accountability

06:55 March to training site or take bus there

07:30 Daily skills training

11:45 Formation for accountability

12:00 Lunch

12:20 Formation for accountability

12:30 More skills daily training

15:00 Formation for accountability

15:30 March back to barracks or take bus there

16:05 Formation for accountability

16:20 Barracks clean up/police call

17:00 Formation for accountability

17:20 Dinner

17:45 Formation for accountability

18:00 Barracks maintenance

18:45 Mail call/ free time

19:45 Formation for accountability

20:00 Final brief from drill sergeants

20:15 Lights out

Over the four-month training period, we learned all the basic stuff, such as the Uniform Code of Military Justice (UCMJ) and the Army Values (Loyalty, Duty, Respect, Selfless Service, Honor, Integrity, and Personal Courage). With backs straight and faces like flint, we marched in cadence as a platoon, responding to Drill & Ceremony (D&C) commands. As my body adjusted to clunking around in boots, helmet, and heavy body armor, I often felt like a Roman centurion.

As cavalry scouts, we received a broad range of combat skills training aimed at preparing us for operating behind enemy lines. These included escape and evasion, hand-to-hand combat, reconnaissance, gathering and reporting information, map and compass use, communications, medical response, familiarization with equipment, and standard operation procedures during active deployment.

Reflecting on all this instruction, Ryans said, "This will sound crazy, but I've never felt as well served in my life as I did at basic training. We recruits were at the receiving end of a tremendous amount of resources. It was amazing how much infrastructure was involved, and how many hours of planning and pre-training the drill sergeants did for every session we experienced. In a way, I didn't feel worthy of all the American might, equipment, technology that we handled. Often, I felt like the other guys were just jackasses like me, but we all knew that we were plugged into a magnificent system."

As one might expect, we did a lot of shooting practice at Fort Knox. We focused primarily on the M16-A2 assault rifle, but also handled a range of other weapons. Spending hours on end at shooting ranges gave me the first chance to be outdoors at length since childhood. It was nice just to absorb the fresh winter air. Ryans felt the same way. He said, "Spending time outside, seeing the seasons change from winter to spring, was magical. It was great to see everything turning green and all the wildflowers blooming. Never before did I appreciate and almost fall in love with seasonal allergies."

The shooting range was lovely at night, because night-time fire meant *tracers!* Tracers are bullets that burn brightly, so shooters can see their trajectories in the dark. When shot in large volumes, they create a magnificent light show as they fly downrange, spiraling off in crazy directions upon ricocheting. It's one of those things you have to see firsthand to understand. Naturally, outgoing tracers are a lot more fun to watch than ones coming at you. Trying to write about it, I asked a number of friends for their own descriptions or photos to convey the effect, but my buddy Boysie Turner (an Irish Guards officer in Britain) dismissed the effort, saying "it's impossible for photographs to do justice to the real thing."

In our basic training world of suspended adolescence, marksmanship assumed the same role as other stupid metrics in life—such as how much money you have, or how much you can bench press—as shorthand for assessing one's competence. After each session on the range, everyone's most recent shooting score immediately became a substitute for his total value as a human being. It was hilarious to watch how the guys who shot well would run around asking everyone else what their scores were, hoping for the chance to boast in response, while those who shot badly would slink around hang-dog trying to avoid eye contact. My own scores varied enough from day to day that I experienced both the highs and the lows of this emotional rollercoaster.

In addition to shooting at ranges, we learned to move and shoot under fire by using "three second rushes." That is, when you're advancing against an enemy, you crawl on the ground for a while, then spring up, sprint forward for the amount of time it takes to say to yourself "I'm up; he sees me; I'm down," and then dive back to the ground. We rehearsed these methods at the Combat Movement course, inching across a football field of mulch (designed for the purpose) with helmets and cheeks pressed down into the ground as the drill sergeants sprayed us with garden hoses. They really kicked into comedic high gear on this occasion, making fun of us to each other as we floundered around. One drill sergeant kept shouting, "There's no place like home! There's no place like home!" like Dorothy in *The Wizard of Oz*. To one sad sack, he shouted, "Private, on your feet!" The private sprang up. "Click your heels three times and think of home." The private pathetically tried to click his heels together in the mud. The sergeant beamed a smile, and then with a straight face, he shook his head and said, "Didn't work, Prive. You're *still* here."

With the Iraq and Afghanistan wars raging that February in 2005, some of our drill sergeants and cadre were recent veterans fresh from combat. Many had been with the historic "Brave Rifles," 3rd Cavalry Regiment, which had just helped spearhead the Iraq invasion. As blooded soldiers, most of them were not cocky. Many treated us with compassion because they knew what might await us overseas.

Quite memorably, one of the cadre sergeants demonstrated how to use our rifles to push and shove when dealing with an angry mob. He said, "Use the weight of your gear and body armor for leverage to push people back. If someone gets violent, jam the muzzle of your weapon, like this [he did a bayonet thrusting motion] into his trachea." The veterans deadpanned such advice not so much with bluster and bravado, but with hard remorse.

One of the main things they stressed the need for "force and violence of action." They insisted that in combat, instantaneous aggression would usually determine an engagement's outcome more than anything else. One said, "When facing an enemy or a threat, decide what to do and then DOT IT with FULL COMMITMENT. NEVER HESITATE. Violent action without hesitation will decide a situation before it ever develops." I've mulled over this ever since. It's a concept that civilian life could never have taught me, and it validated my expectation that the army would help round out my liberal arts education.

Another cadre sergeant seemed like he was riding a high from his recent deployment. He treated the whole thing like a joke, telling us that whenever his Humvee crew was about to engage in a firefight during the Iraq invasion, he would blast the 1980s Boy George song, *Do You Really Want to Hurt Me* on a stereo inside the vehicle. Considering that normal army preference would deem heavy metal or rap the more acceptable forms of music for such occasions, his eccentricity made me chortle with delight.

Fully expecting to deploy to the Middle East, we took all these stories at face value, without any grains of salt. I was impressed by how the younger soldiers in our platoon processed their expectations of going to war. One day, I overheard two privates (each about 18 years old) pragmatically discussing how they would manage in life if they ended up losing an arm or leg in combat.

Thoughts about death and physical injury brought questions about God to the surface that had been dormant for years. It might sound cliché to say "there are no atheists in foxholes," but that doesn't make it any less true. As a kid, I used to hate sitting through church, but at Fort Knox it seemed like a privilege. Most of the guys went to the general Protestant worship or Catholic mass, but Ryans and I chose the Episcopalian route. The chaplain there was a kindly man who actually believed in the Bible (a seeming rarity among Episcopal clergy). And just as crucially, he served cookies after each service. When singing familiar hymns, my eyes would involuntarily stream with tears, which wasn't surprising. My mother and I (Mom was raised Presbyterian) had always been unabashed hymn criers. Years later, I mentioned this in passing to my grandmother. She got embarrassed, looked both ways to make sure none of her compatriots at the retirement home were listening and whispered "It's fine to tell me that you cry in church, dear, but don't let anyone else know! We need you to at least *seem* emotionally stable." What empathy my grandmother lacked, the drill sergeants had. They tended to be very nice when driving us to and from church on Sundays.

We all dreaded Gas Chamber Day, yet another initiation rite. For weeks in advance, the drill sergeants showed us how to use our protective masks in response to poison gas attacks. On Gas Day, they filed us into a sealed-off room filled with tear gas for testing. Each of us had to sit still for a few minutes in the gas chamber with our masks on, to

247

show that we could breathe with them. Most soldiers managed this easily enough, but a few luckless individuals abruptly discovered that their masks leaked. They panicked, screaming and shouting, and were escorted quickly outside. Next, we had to allow gas to enter our masks and then expel it by sharply exhaling. Finally, we had to remove our masks completely and inhale the tear gas while reciting the Pledge of Allegiance. After all that, we stumbled outside into the fresh air, blinded, coughing, and gagging. A wave of euphoria then washed it all away as the pain ebbed and the experience was safely in the rear-view mirror.

The happiest point during basic training was Family Weekend, when everyone got a weekend off to spend with visitors from home. It was fascinating (and sobering) for everyone to glimpse of each other's relations up close. For months, our shaved heads, identical uniforms, and groupthink had worked to erase person's individuality. But when the families showed up, I was astounded to see what a polyglot tapestry of modern Americana we actually were. My mom and sister were there smiling, having made a road trip down from Pennsylvania. They were much impressed by our healthy appearance and ruddy outdoor cheeks, and I was charmed to see them trotted out in Barbour jackets and silk scarves. We spent that weekend driving through stunning Kentucky horse country, stopping off at picturesque towns along the way. Sometimes it seemed like rural Pennsylvania except for the accents. I was smitten when a cute girl behind a country drug-store counter gave directions saying "thar" instead of "there."

Now before the drill sergeants released us for family weekend, they *explicitly* said that we were forbidden to either drink alcohol or get tattoos while away. They asked multiple

248

times to make sure every private understood this command. And every private, eager to get the hell out of Fort Knox, firmly assented.

Apparently, the drill sergeants knew perfectly well from experience that some privates would disobey these orders, so the moment we returned, they had us strip down for a tattoo inspection. I never considered getting a tattoo, so I thought nothing of it. The next day however, during lunch break at the motor pool, I noticed the drill sergeants forming a huddle, laughing and congratulating each other, which immediately raised my antennae. Something sinister had to be afoot.

Suddenly, the wittiest and cruelest of them—a short, stocky, bald-headed Chicago street tough whose great native intelligence was uncorrupted by formal education—climbed onto a tank and read off a list of names, smiling to himself as he did so. As he snapped off each name, the associated private leapt to his feet and reluctantly shuffled up to the tank. The drill sergeant then proclaimed that we were going to have a little *fashion show*.

He announced that these particular privates demonstrated how "special" they were by getting tattoos on family weekend. He crowed, "If these privates were so eager to disobey a direct order from their Commanding Officer, then their tattoos must have really been worth it! They must be the coolest, most bad-assed tattoos known to man." Turning to the privates, he said, "Now, why don't you jump up on this tank and let us all take a look at your amazing taste in body art?" One by one, each man climbed up on the tank and stripped to reveal his offending image. Each hapless private had chosen the most macho tattoo he could find, many of them containing would-be cavalry themes, with saber and horse motifs paired with skulls, dragons and flames, etc. Imitating art connoisseurs at a gallery or auction house, the drill sergeants clustered around each private, critiquing the nuances of each tattoo for minutes on end—minutes (for the privates at least) which must surely have seemed like hours. The sergeants outdid each other, spinning off one hilarious analogy after another in piercing banter. It was theatre worthy of any stage in New York or London. I laughed so hard the muscles in my face and stomach seized up with lactic acid.

Though four months of basic hazing at Fort Knox passed slowly, it all mercifully came to an end. John Bansemer had been right: "Basic training is like pink eye. It sucks, and then it's over." After handing in our equipment piece by piece (a process that took days) and holding a final graduation ceremony, we went our separate ways and flew home.

Walking through the airport, dressed in the Class-A uniform, with shaved head, I was thrilled with new appreciation for things like drinking coffee, reading books, wandering around on my own, listening to music, sleeping in, and driving a car. I learned a valuable lesson—something you might call "reverse luxury." You can make life more luxurious not by acquiring new comforts, but rather by abstaining from things you've always taken for granted.

# Chapter 32

# Learning to Ride

Once I was home from Fort Knox, I finally felt like a full-fledged First City Trooper. At the Radnor Hunt Races that year a number of older guys wandered up to introduce themselves, comment on my shaved head, and ask if I was a Trooper just back from basic training. Their handshakes (and a few of Jim Tornetta's delicious Pine Valleys—brewed in a galvanized steel garbage can with ice and mint leaves left out in the sun) made me thankful to have left Heidelberg to join the gentlemen of Gloucester.

Now it was time to learn to ride horses. I say "horses" in the plural, because a cavalry scout is traditionally expected to ride any mount. True to its Gloucester fox-hunting origins, the old equestrian spirit remained strong within the unit. With National Guard drills one weekend each month and riding practices once a week, it was still possible for a modern Trooper could spend more hours per year on a horse than in a military vehicle.

Having not been born to the saddle, I initially expected to have a rocky learning curve. But weekly lessons at Valley Forge Military Academy were fairly easy. It was intimidating at first to tack up a horse, lead the beast clip-clopping out of its stall (and have it step on your foot once or twice), swing a leg over the saddle, and then start off on a slow walk around the ring. Each riding lesson included dressage, walking, trotting, cantering, and going over modest jumps. Sometimes we practiced cavalry skills such as tent-pegging (described in an earlier chapter) or doing knightly things like trying to snag a hanging ring with a lance while cantering.

Our paid instructor back then was an old polo coach who took a dim view of our abilities. Toward the end of each session, he would sort of give up, and try to get out of teaching by telling us to spend the rest of the evening playing tag on horseback. Dodging around the ring on a nimble quarter horse polo pony, I learned more from playing tag than I did from his instruction.

Riding supplemented our military training in countless "character building" ways. For one thing, it instilled raw physical courage much more than army training did, because horses are dangerous. As easy as it is to mount one, it's just as easy to dismount involuntarily—and at speed. Horses can sense a rider's confidence and can feel how a rider's stomach muscles tighten or how he is breathing. Like naughty kids (or lazy privates in the Army), horses attempt to test their riders to see what they can get away with. If they sense fear or hesitancy, they take advantage of it. Because they are animals of flight, it's essential to keep them calm, confident, and fearless.

Horse riding required something the Germans call "Selbstbeherrshung" and what we English speakers call "self-command." (For obvious cultural reasons, the concept always seemed to have extra kick whenever I thought of it in German.) Horses forced me to master myself in the most mundane ways. For example, each time I walked into a paddock (a small field or enclosure where horses are kept) to fetch my horse, I had to behave very calmly. Instead of just barging in, I had to open the gate slowly, shut it behind me softly, and then walk with confidence through the field past all the other horses (who at any time might spook, bit, or kick) to locate mine, and bridle it up even if it didn't want to be bridled.

Another lesson was situational foresight. To stay in the saddle, a rider must constantly think a few steps ahead of his horse. As a fox hunter once told me, "You have to make constant adjustments when hunting. You must anticipate what's coming and use constant imperceptible adjustments to get the horse there. The adjustments come from the slightest hints and pressure, whether through the hands, seat, or breathing." From a military standpoint, those same skills come in very handy when leading men.

Horses also schooled us in clarity—the need to avoid giving mixed signals. This came to light one time when I got thrown from a horse when trying to take it over a low jump. Our instructor pulled me aside afterward and said,

"You didn't get thrown off. You merely got bumped off! Why? Because you got nervous right before the jump and pulled back on the reins, asking him to slow up. At the same time, you squeezed him with your heels to ask him to make the jump. You gave him two conflicting signals based on your own lack of confidence, and he obeyed. He took the jump, but he also slowed up, and in slowing up, his gait bumped you right out of the saddle. If you learn to take the jumps with full commitment—not holding back—you'll send one message, not two. The horse will then find its own way over the jump."

What marvelous advice! With time, I found myself applying these equestrian skills to human relationships, adding a little Selbstbeherrschung along the way. On later occasions, when entering a business meeting, approaching a girl at a cocktail party, or doing foot patrols as a soldier in Iraq, I would slow down my breathing, calmly put one foot in front of the other, and pretend that I was walking into a paddock.

*The author, having just learned to ride (attempting to act poised in the saddle), directs traffic at the Border Plate while his father furtively tries to steer clear in the background. (Photo by Alix Cummin)*

# Chapter 33

# Annual Dinners and Church Service

By tradition, the Troop celebrates three annual events that kick off with full-dress horse rides through center city Philadelphia. These include the unit's Anniversary dinner, George Washington's birthday dinner, and George Washington's commemorative church service. My first exposure to these customs as a new Trooper left vivid impressions.

It's quite an experience to trot down Chestnut Street on rented horses with a dozen other guys in Napoleonic dress, bouncing around on the saddle at the seated trot with helmet, saber, and baldric box all rattling aflutter, knowing that anyone who falls off his horse or loses a piece of equipment while mounted must buy the Troop a case of champagne. I always found it a full time job to keep the towering bearskin helmet on my head from falling off. Stuffed with a t-shirt for padding, it sat on my head without quite fitting, and required me to jut my jaw out against the chin strap to keep it from getting knocked off by cross winds at intersections. Riding through town past onlookers was like running a gauntlet. Women gave catcalls. Homeless people shouted nonsensical compliments or insults.

*Troopers march through center city Philadelphia to celebrate another anniversary dinner. Each year they ride from the Armory to Carpenter's Hall and back, with a brief layover at the Philadelphia Club. (Photo by Ryan Noyes)*

After riding through town, we returned to the Armory where Non-active and Honorary Troopers had been gathering to greet us with cheers and applause. Climbing the steps to the mess hall for dinner was a strictly choreographed affair. Active Roll members lined the main stairway in descending order, with the most recent members (those with the highest Troop numbers) standing at the bottom and the most senior members at the top, signing Troop songs all the while. Youngsters and old boys alike—aged 18 to 80 (and older)—sang in unison as they made their way upstairs past the photos and paintings, shaking hands along the way. Emotions seemed to run high as people greeted old friends, remarking about how much the Troop has changed over the years, and how much it remained the same.

Up in the mess hall, dramatically illuminated by candle light, battle standards, guidons, and portraits look down from the walls with benign approval. Before anyone could sit down to eat, the room was called to attention as the color guard marched in with flags for the United States, the Troop, and the nation of the visiting Boyer Scholar. After the chaplain offered a prayer, a Junior Troopers read out the name of each unit member killed in action since 1774. At that point, I wasn't sure whether I was in a British cavalry regiment, or a Philadelphia social club with a long mortality list.

We newly elected Troopers now had to walk around the room with silver "loving cups" (three-handled jugs that are passed between two people facing each other). The cups were filled with champagne, each cup commemorating one of the Troop's deployments. As we went through the entire room, each of us had to drink a toast with everyone in the unit as a pledge of brotherhood. To each man, I had to extend the following invitation: "Sir, will you drink with me to the honor of the Troop?" He then had to snap to attention and reply, "Sir, it would be a privilege! To the honor of the Troop!"

*A new member passes the loving cup, "to the honor of the Troop." (First City Troop collection)*

Throughout dinner, Troopers of all ages stood on their chairs to belt out more songs, the older men hobbling up on their chairs with the nervous help from friends. Many of them howled out witty and complicated numbers written decades earlier at annual training.

*(Previous page and below) Anniversary dinner snapshots.*
*(Photos from First City Troop collection; James Blunt)*

As dinner wrapped up, cigars and coffee were distributed. Catering waitresses came in to clear the tables and the Active Roll stood up to help them in their work. By tradition, Troopers always assist the staff because we are all servants equally. Downstairs, many people chattered away in the NCO Club for the rest of the night, some of them remaining until dawn.

*NCO Club after an Anniversary Dinner. (Photo by Ryan Noyes)*

259

Wearing the Troop's full dress uniform is a tradition unto itself. Each new man who joins the unit receives his uniform from available stock, and getting all the right gear was a crap shoot. When I joined in 2004 for example, the quartermaster handed me a tunic that had been hand-tailored in the 1930s—and smelled that way. The collar was split and separating. One of the epaulettes would only stay on with safety pins. However, the trousers were brand spanking new, custom ordered to my own measurements. Each year, the quartermaster ordered one or two new pieces but kept old items until they were in shreds. Some of our heavy woolen capes, used only during the coldest weather and beautifully made, dated from 1912!

Before World War II, each Trooper would have to buy his own uniform at great personal expense. But after the war, the quartermaster assembled enough hand-me-downs to lend them out to Active Roll for free, like books from a library. That uniform stock has been maintained on an on-going basis ever since. Mended uniforms keep circulating until they disintegrate into rags—which is not a bad metaphor for the First City Troop itself.

Whatever concerns I had about our uniforms' ratty conditions evaporated one night when a British colonel came to an anniversary dinner. Resplendent in his regimentals, from a distance the man looked immaculate. However, up close, I gleefully observed that his uniform was hardly better than mine. His trouser cuffs were frayed over the boot heels, and one of his epaulettes suspiciously looked like it had been attached with a safety pin.

In addition to the Lafayette-designed full dress uniform, Troopers also wear Mess Dress. Mess dress is the military equivalent of black tie/ dinner jacket/ tuxedo. By tradition, Troopers usually get their own mess dress uniforms made to measure and then, as Tony Morris quaintly put it, "donate them back to the Troop upon the wearer's demise." Junior Troopers keep an eye peeled for such opportunities. Walking by the Adjutant Farley's office one day, I noticed a mess jacket draped on a chair that a Trooper had just donated. I asked whose it was and Farley said, "might as well take it for yourself. Possession is nine tenths of the law."

*Full Dress, Mounted. (First City Troop collection)*

*Full Dress, Dismounted. (First City Troop collection)*

*Mess Dress. (Photo from Max von Mettenheim)*

The amazing continuity of Troop custom extended not just through the Troop's uniforms, but into their *storage*. Generations ago, uniforms were stored in an empty space between two walls, accessible only through a large hole in the one wall. This space was called "the hole in the wall," for obvious reasons. Since that time, the uniforms have been kept in various other rooms, but each subsequent room has always been called The Hole in the Wall.

In addition to the Anniversary and Washington dinners, the Troop gathers annually for worship at a church service that has mourned President Washington's passing since 1799. The service alternates each year between Christ Church and St. Peter's, the two churches that Washington attended in Philadelphia. Like the two dinners, the church service is highly choreographed, and was fascinating to behold the first time I experienced it. After riding our horses through center city from the Armory, we marched Christ Church singing *Onward Christian Soldiers*, as members of the Orpheus Club (the oldest men's singing club in the United States) sang in accompaniment from the balcony above.

Members of the extended Troop family were well in attendance, smartly dressed in Anglo-American town-and-country fashions. Many had been attending this service for years, regardless of their current involvement with the unit. As Alix Cummin said, "It's a cornerstone event for me each Christmas. As a kid, it was sometimes a drag to sit through church a second time on that Sunday, but it was great when the horses came and the collation followed afterward. The Troop church service and the Orpheus concert mean more and more to me as I get older as I see people from my parents' generation dying, and as my sons are growing up."

When I joined the Troop, the church service took on special solemnity because we faced imminent deployments to the Middle East. Chaplain Clayton Ames took his spiritual responsibility very seriously, saying, "The annual church service is the culmination of a year spent on my part deep in prayer for the spiritual health and eternal destiny of all members of the Troop family. Every time we sing *For All the Saints*, I shower the pulpit with my tears."

*George Washington memorial service at Christ Church or St. Peter's (above). Dougherty family smiles at post-church-service collation (below). (Photos by Alix Cummin)*

Like the Border Plate and the Daughters Ball, the Church Service emphasizes subtle aspects of Philadelphia tradition, taste, and manners that rarely come into view. Nathaniel Burt thought about this culture a great deal, and his views bear some emphasis. He said, "At its best, and within its limits, the social temperature of Philadelphia is almost perfect... There is a natural, relaxed, live-and-let-live about Philadelphia taste and manners that demands nothing of you but an equal simplicity and casualness." He defined Philadelphia taste as a balance between two opposite poles— the *plain* and the *fancy*—which characterized Philadelphia's elite back in colonial times. For generations, the region was dominated by Quakers and Anglicans (more accurately, Quakers who became Anglican). Their tastes combined a Quaker love of plainness, modesty, and simplicity with an Anglican love of pageantry, opulence, and "good form" (unwritten assumptions about what is and isn't "done"), which have remained ingrained in Philadelphia ever since... I could go on and on about this dynamic, but it's probably best to leave it at that for now.

*Troopers, friends, and family sing Christmas carols on Rittenhouse Square. (Photo by Ryan Noyes)*

# Chapter 34

# Iraq

Within a year after I returned from Fort Knox, nine Troopers were sent to Iraq under the command of Bravo Troop, one of our sister units in the squadron. Although I would like to have interviewed each of those Troopers for this book, not enough time has passed for me to be ready to talk to them about it in full depth.

Tom Farley was one of the nine men who volunteered to go. Although he was 58 years old and had already served in Vietnam and Bosnia, he felt like he still had a deployment left in him. He said, "I enjoyed Vietnam and I felt like I could still do stuff." To get his fiancé Cathe's approval, he told her, "I have to go to Iraq," which she interpreted to mean that he was being made to go, but his "having to go" came instead from the inside.

Farley said that his group's train-up for Iraq was miserable and long, lasting six full months—the same amount of time that a Marine unit would normally spend "in country." He was excited though, because he knew they were heading for Ramadi, the center of fighting at the time. The media referred to Ramadi as the most dangerous place in the world.

Farley said, "Iraq put your teeth on edge because at any moment something big could blow up real close to you. That was on your mind all the time." While in Ramadi, he carved a niche for himself on the midnight communications shift in the TOC, as "the voice in the night for all the guys out there in sector." He volunteered for patrols outside the wire whenever possible. Describing these operations, he said, "I didn't feel a sense of imminent battle for tactical firefights like we had in Vietnam. Instead, I had the sense of imminent danger that at any moment, something could blow up. From what we were told, the battle of Fallujah had been a real inner-city pain in the ass, but the Marines said Ramadi was worse." He noticed that the men who went out on operations every day changed a great deal. "Their outlook about the world changed over time. Imperceptibly, after a couple of months, you looked at a person, and he was a different person."

*Andrew Colket just returned from patrol to Camp Ramadi (above). Thomas Werner on patrol in Ramadi province (below). (Photos from Andrew Colket and Thomas Werner)*

Soon, I would be joining them.

One morning in October 2005, as I was stepping out of the shower at my parents' house in Collegeville (a Philadelphia exurb), I got a phone call. It was John Faller, my buddy from Basic Training. He was hanging out at the Armory. He said, "Meschter, the guys in Ramadi have taken a lot of casualties apparently. Squadron is looking for volunteers to go over as replacements. They hope single guys will go so married guys won't have to. There's a long list of people I need to call about this, but I wanted to give you a heads up right away, to see if you're interested."

A surge of adrenaline shot through me. I didn't want to give him an answer straight away, so I said, "I'm going to drive into town to the Armory right now. It will take an hour with traffic. I'll think about this in the car. By the time I get there, I will give you an answer." As I drove down the Schuylkill Expressway in my Honda Civic, thoughts flooded my head about what I'd just learned at basic training less than a year earlier. I knew what modern weapons could do to people. I recalled the first aid training for how to treat burns, amputated limbs, and gas attacks. I recalled how machine guns kicked as you fired them, the smell of the cartridges, the concussion of grenades and artillery, and the expressions on the faces of the Iraq veterans assigned to train us. There were plenty of reasons not to volunteer. But as my tires crossed into the Armory's portico, I knew firmly that I had to go. Or rather, I couldn't *not* go. I walked into the readiness NCO's office, knocked on his glass door, and told Staff Sergeant Heyman to count me in. Heyman seemed shocked, probably because he didn't think of me as soldier material. Just a month earlier, he yelled at me for addressing him as "Dude" while in uniform.

After a few months of bureaucratic delay that I was perfectly happy with, I went to Camp Shelby, Mississippi, for training. That region had recently been hit by Hurricane Katrina. Downed trees and damaged buildings were everywhere, but the smashed up sugar pines gave the woods a delightful scent.

Upon arrival, I felt a dull sense of panic as I plunged back into Army mode so soon after basic training. A powerful sense of loneliness and fear swept over me, but it soon became obvious that everyone else was also afraid. Mutual fear seemed to curb my loneness as everyone seemed to realize that we were all in the same boat. Like a tonic, fear stripped away bravado, which made it easier to make friends. There was no room for faking it when you really might not be coming back.

Barracks life was also a tonic. Up to then, I'd always enjoyed the extremes of either luxurious or ascetic living. Although before joining the Army I'd lived in Durham and Heidelberg (two sumptuously charming cities), at Camp Shelby, I was often happier than I'd ever been in Europe. The basicness of it put me at ease. I enjoyed the unpainted concrete-block barracks, cement floors, simple toilet fixtures streaked with rust, and naked light bulbs screwed into the ceiling sockets. All my possessions fit into a duffle bag and wall locker. I wore the same uniform each day, carrying the same essential personal items (wallet, cell phone, Leatherman Wave multi-tool) in the same exact pockets. Army food at the chow hall was always good, always free, and you never had to clean up afterward.

Across the street, we had an Enlisted Man's Club and a gym. After final formation each day, our entire platoon would run to the club like kids let out for recess. At night, I read books, with one ear cocked to the hilarious banter of guys (some of them bright and some moronic) in the barracks. Who knew what waited in Iraq? I thought, "This experience might make me stronger as a person or it might kill me." I was comfortable facing either outcome but not with getting injured or maimed for life. I often ran into soldiers at the EM Club who were on their way back from Iraq on leave, who told horror stories about Ramadi. One man referred to it as a "meat grinder." Each of them said we were crazy for having volunteered. To prepare myself mentally, I read numerous combat memoirs such as *With the Old Breed* by Eugene Sledge and *Storm of Steel* by Ernst Juenger, a few self-help books about Stoicism and Zen Buddhism, and meditated each night on Oswald Chambers's *My Utmost for His Highest*, a Christian devotional.

The training at Camp Shelby was similar to Fort Knox, but whereas basic training at Fort Knox was designed to break recruits down, deployment training was meant to build soldiers up. Our trainers treated us with compassion, knowing that some of us might not come back.

Surprisingly, I found that I enjoyed urban operations training more than anything else, even though it's one of the more nerve-wracking forms of combat. We learned how to enter a building in four-man "stack teams." Four men would line up outside the front door, each man leaning all his weight into the man in front of him, while the lead man pushed all his weight back, which forced all four men to become a coiled spring. The instant the door got breached, the whole stack team piled into the house at once. Each man covered a pre-assigned sector in order to cover every part of each room as it was entered. We learned to maneuver through buildings, how to navigate corners and stairs, and how to stay away from the walls, to keep from being hit by stray bullets. The most valuable lesson I learned from Urban Operations training was the mantra "slow equals smooth, and smooth equals fast." In other words, the way to perfect a complex task is to rehearse each individual part very slowly. Then, when all the parts are mastered, they can be integrated into one smooth movement.

Along the way, I befriended a guy in our platoon called Bill, who came from Los Angeles. An aging rock band musician, he had been a private in the first Iraq war. He was a charming and irresponsible ne'er-do-well who spoke like a surfer and whose aging adolescent good looks often made women think they could reform him (always to their disappointment). We got along well.

On the rifle range one day, Bill's face lit up. He said, "Duuude, let's volunteer to load tracers in the ammo shed so we can load everyone's magazine with twice the amount of tracer rounds they're supposed to get. Then we'll kick back tonight and watch the fireworks." This was a weak point for me. The reader may recall my affinity for night time tracer fire. I required no arm twisting. We dove into our task with boyish glee, straining every muscle to keep straight faces as we handed soldier after soldier a double dose of tracers. To reward ourselves for all that hard work, we loaded our own magazines entirely with tracers.

When nighttime firing commenced, the results were spectacular. The bullets arced, whizzed, and spiraled in every direction. The range NCOs knew that something wasn't quite right, but no one stopped the shooting. After a while, however, people started smelling smoke, and the smoke seemed to come from the wood line. Soon there wasn't just smoke, but the glow of a forest fire. Range fires occurred quite often, so this wasn't such an odd occurrence. They called in firefighters and shut down the range. The firefighters and the range officers weren't going to Iraq, and they weren't running the same risks we were, so we felt no remorse for giving them some extra work that night. When we got to Iraq a few weeks later, Bill and I wound up in different units, which was probably for the best. I later heard that while fooling around with a smoke grenade, he accidentally ignited it and dropped it into the hatch of his own vehicle.

After a long series of airplane flights and tedious layovers stretching from Mississippi to Maine to Germany to Kuwait, I found myself sitting on the floor of an armored truck in Iraq, driving northward to Ramadi. A bunch of us were crammed in, sprawled out and weighed down with weapons, battle gear, and body armor. The truck bed had thick armored plates welded to the sides, and the Marines had given us strict instructions not to poke our heads up to look around. They warned, "You'll be shot by snipers if you do." For hours, my sensory input was limited to the sound of the motor and a patch of brilliant blue sky overhead. After bouncing around on rough roads, the truck finally squealed to a stop, and the steel gate swung open. When I stood up, stretched, and scanned the horizon, what I saw took my breath away. In every direction for miles there stretched a vast sea of mud, sprinkled with a million silver puddles, reflecting the twilight sky.

*Author lounges on a stack of duffle bags (meticulously adjusted to achieve zero-gravity comfort) during one of the many staging areas in transit. Soldiers make themselves comfortable however they can. (Author's photo)*

Camp Ramadi was nicknamed Ra-muddy for good reason. Its fine, powdery clay soil liquefied with rain. Wooden pallets that were laid out to form walkways sank so deeply into the mud that, even when you walked on them, the muck was ankle deep. Upon arrival, a sergeant informed a handful of us that we would not serve with the soldiers from Philadelphia as intended but that instead we were assigned to a combat-engineering platoon from Rhode Island attached to an infantry company. This news instantly altered the sort of tour I expected to have. Instead of spending time patrolling highways by vehicle as a cavalry scout, I would wander around on foot as an infantryman. A perverse part of me was thrilled about this, however. I had always wanted to experience war as an infantryman. Admittedly, that desire had been sharpest while reading books about war on distant campus park benches, listening to chirping birds.

*Camp Ramadi, when the puddles dried out. (Author's photo)*

Entering a seasoned combat unit as a "replacement" is supposed to be an alienating experience, just a notch easier perhaps than being the new guy in prison. I braced myself for rough treatment but found everyone surprisingly nice at first. When the soldiers from our new platoon came to pick us up, they looked haggard. Their aging vehicles, the same Vietnam-era Armored Personnel Carriers (APCs) that we used on drill weekends back in Pennsylvania, gave me a sense of comfort. We climbed into the vehicles, stowed our gear, and rolled out. The main gate at Camp Ramadi was a Paladin self-propelled howitzer that simply rolled back and forth in front of an opening in the wall. As we left the camp and turned right onto a country road, the sergeant next to me stood up in the vehicle's troop hatch, surrounded by sandbags and welded plates of "hillbilly armor" for protection against snipers and

Improvised Explosive Devices (IEDs). He pulled a scarf up over his mouth, gave me a weapon, and told me to stand up with him to pull security. He handed me a magazine that was heavy with live ammunition. I felt the weight of it in my hand before slapping it into the magazine well, thinking, "This is the first time I've ever held a loaded a weapon for use against humans."

Ramshackle buildings lined one side of the road. As I strained to scan the rooftops, windows, and foliage, my mind boggled at how many hiding places and vantage points an enterprising insurgent had from which to shoot us. We crossed a bridge over a swollen pewter-gray river no wider than the Schuylkill River back home. The fast-moving water looked filthy, but for some reason it was also alluring. As I was wondering about the river, the sergeant tapped me on the shoulder and shouted through his scarf that this was the Euphrates. It gave me a shudder to think that this was Mesopotamia, the Cradle of Civilization, the place mentioned in the Book of Revelation when God says, "Loose the four angels who are bound in the great river Euphrates."

We then entered Camp Blue Diamond, which would be our home. It had once been Uday Hussein's palace compound. Good old Uday. As a member of the Iraq Olympic Committee, he kept a private torture scorecard for how many times each football player should be beaten on the soles of his feet for underperforming. Marines and Navy SEALs also used the camp as their base of operations. Blue Diamond was smaller than Camp Ramadi and much nicer. While Ramadi was a vast mud flat, sprawled with overcrowded buildings and devoid of trees, Blue Diamond had a tidy-village feel to it, with paved roads, sweetly scented shade trees, and a chow hall rumored to be the best in Iraq. As all this dawned on me, I thought, "Blue

Diamond isn't just across the river from Ramadi, it's across the *tracks.*"

*Camp Blue Diamond, the other side of the tracks—a "Garden of Eden" compared with Camp Ramadi. (Author's photo)*

My future squad leader came up to greet me, and then took a step back. "You a college boy, Meschter?" he asked. "Yes, Sergeant," I answered. In response, he snapped, "So that means you think you're better than me!?" This was neither the first nor the last time that I would wrangle with a blue-collar chip-on-the-shoulder in the Army. Such altercations are the First City Trooper's natural lot. It's the Trooper's responsibility to respond humbly while also standing up to potential bullies— a delicate balancing act.

Though I tried to blend in, there were times when my judgment failed abysmally. For example, I bought a beautiful Ashton brier pipe online and had it sent to me in Iraq. The morning after it arrived, I brought it along in my cargo pocket on our daily patrol. As we assembled in the motor pool for our normal mission brief, some guys pulled out cigarettes like normal, so I pulled out my new pipe. After getting a good draw on it, clouds of delightfully scented tobacco wafted over our platoon in the morning sun. Pipe firmly clenched in teeth, I was busy focusing my attention on what the platoon sergeant was telling us, when my best friend in the platoon quietly stepped behind me and hissed in my ear, "*Meschter!* How on earth do you have the balls to smoke a fucking pipe in front of these guys at a mission brief?" At that, I looked around and realized that a good number of them seemed to want to take my head off. I finished smoking the pipe as casually as I could and then put it in my pocket, never to bring it out again.

Camp Blue Diamond might have been pleasant compared to Camp Ramadi, but my personal living quarters left much to be desired. Eight of us were crammed in a small room. The windows, long ago sealed off by sandbags to prevent shrapnel from entering, kept out both sunlight and fresh air. Each man had a full bunk bed. This allowed us to throw gear onto one mattress and sleep on the other. The place reeked from body armor and boots that had been worn for months in 100-degree heat and never washed. Personal equipment, weapons, uniforms, dirty and clean laundry, food wrappers, and other detritus filled each man's sleeping area. I adjusted easily enough to all this, my tolerance for squalor being quite high.

*A snapshot of the author's barracks in Iraq. It's a good thing that pictures can't convey smell. (Author's photo)*

Within two days, I experienced my first foot patrol. We formed up at the main gate and stepped off in a staggered column, a tactical walking formation, to prevent men from bunching too close together in case of attack. We patrolled at an easy walking pace toward the neighboring village. This was first time I ever walked somewhere knowing that there were people out there who wanted to kill me. A guard had been shot in one of the watchtowers just recently. At first, I was acutely aware of my footsteps, thinking that each one could be the last. Then, some passages from Psalm 91 came to mind from the Bible. My mom used to read that particular psalm to me when I had nightmares about rattlesnakes as a child. "You will tread on the lion and the cobra," she would say aloud (I couldn't read yet). "You will trample the great lion and the serpent." In an earlier verse, she had read, "A thousand may fall at your side, ten thousand at your right hand, but it will not come near you. ...Only with your eyes will you see the destruction of the wicked." That seemed to offer the promise of protection in war.

*Combat engineer platoon on foot patrol in a staggered column.*
*(Photo by Christopher Pollard)*

Psalm 91's promises, which as a child I took literally but which in my younger adult years I had assumed to be mere poetry, suddenly seemed applicable to my immediate situation. I asked myself, "Are the promises in Psalm 91 literal or figurative?" As I walked on, outfitted with my Kevlar helmet, combat earplugs, ballistic sunglasses, heavy body armor, and weapon with laser sight locked, loaded, and held at the low-ready, I felt the gravel crunching beneath each footstep. I scanned 360 degrees for signs of the enemy and found myself accepting the following life-changing assumption: "The promises in Psalm 91 (and the whole Bible by extension) are literal enough for me to bet my safety in combat and my life after death on them." Suddenly, a burden fell from me and I continued that patrol and every other one after it with a belief in divine providence.

That first patrol passed without incident, as did others in the weeks that followed. On patrols, straining to take in so much visually, I saw the world around me not as a fluid moving picture but rather as a series of quick snapshots: "Click, click,

click, click." I visualized it all like a camera. Those mental snapshots recorded scenes of Iraqi villages, our walking through people's back yards, going through people's houses, jumping over drainage ditches and irrigation canals and, especially, tramping through patches of ground saturated with sheep, goat, and human excrement. That mud stained everyone's boots. Behind the houses were fire pits where the women cooked their bread outdoors, the aroma of bread and charcoal wafting toward us. It was fun to see how the local Iraqis lived. It oddly felt like armed tourism, almost like living in a National Geographic magazine article.

Part of our mission required us to poke through people's houses in search of weapons or insurgents. Most of us felt embarrassed to have to go through their homes. The sergeants tried to be super courteous, like kids visiting friends' parents' houses. They would constantly say, "Please," and "Thank you," over-emphasizing each word. An Iraqi interpreter accompanied us. Each time we entered a house, my squad leader would tell me to go upstairs to the roof, to pull security. I would cautiously round each corner, with my weapon at the ready and my finger on the trigger, and work my way upstairs to the roof. The house layouts were interesting. Instead of tables or chairs, they had colorful cushions and rugs used for sitting directly on the floor. The people in this village were not rich. Therefore, the houses were simply decorated and pleasantly understated. We often gave candy to Iraqi kids, which always made me feel acutely American, like the GIs in World War II, dispensing Hershey bars and nylons. Sometimes we brought soccer balls to hand out, but we stopped when we noticed that it led to bullying. I once saw a little kid gleefully catch a bouncing soccer ball we tossed to him, only to have the smile wiped away when a much larger kid punched him in the face and took the ball.

*The author looks up while chatting with villagers. (Photo by Christopher Pollard)*

It didn't take long for me to make a new best friend in our platoon. Named Erenberg, he was tall, lean, had a clean-cut face, and didn't say much. We started talking one day, when I noticed a patch on his body armor embroidered with the letters SPQR. I asked him what that meant, and he said, "Senatus Populusque Romanus, the Senate and People of Rome. America is the new Rome, and I'm an imperial grunt." Erenberg was referring to *Imperial Grunts*, a popular book at the time. This casual conversation opened the door for me to hear his fascinating life story. Erenberg had been a Navy SEAL but never saw any combat on active duty. He left the Navy and went to college, where he studied classics and law. He later joined the National Guard to become a Cavalry Scout, reasoning that he was more likely to see combat as a

Guardsman than as a SEAL. On top of all that, he read the *Economist.* In short, he had all the earmarks of a classic First City Trooper.

Navy SEALs operated from our base. We would see them walking around occasionally, and like the cool kids in any high school, they would all sit together at the same tables in chow hall. My closest brush with special operations was when I got to hold the flashlight for a SEAL as he set up some complicated electronic device on a shared mission. Rolling my eyes at myself, I felt as useful as a six-year-old kid helping his dad work on a home-improvement project in the garage.

The ease of our initial patrols was short-lived. We moved to a new sector, forty minutes' drive from camp. This area was more rural and much more dangerous. The insurgents wanted to take a stand there. Each day, we'd park our vehicles in the same place and walk through alfalfa fields into a village. It was mid-spring and beautiful. The sun baked the earth into hard clay. The fields, irrigated by canals, were a vivid bright green. The sky was a deep blue. The canals and blue sky reminded me of Holland. Shepherds walked in the distance but close enough for me to hear bells clanging faintly on the necks of their grazing goats. An occasional stray dog yelped in the distance. None of us spoke when we moved through the fields. The distinctive sounds of foot patrols are still vivid in my memory. Thirty pairs of boots struck the ground in broken cadence, while weapons and gunmetal clattered with the rustling swish of each soldier's personal equipment.

A sniper shot at us almost daily. Once or twice a day, the barely audible crack of a distant rifle report signaled that he was some distance away, and a snap in the air or smack on impact indicated the incoming bullet.

We also occasionally received unfriendly mortar fire. The first time I heard the thump of an enemy mortar was when we were crossing an open field. One sergeant motioned for everyone to get down, and the mortar round exploded nearby. I was surprised at how underwhelming the sound was, just a faint clap, followed by a white puff of dust. The explosion's smallness was deceptive, however; one could remove a man's limbs if nearby.

As we crouched down, we felt the fear. I now understood why men instinctively want to cluster together when they are under fire. I looked over and saw Ward, my buddy who came from Charlie Troop in Pennsylvania. He was younger than me. He had braced his head against the same berm, behind which I was crouching. It was good to make eye contact with him because this was his first time under fire, too. For weeks, not much happened besides those sporadic sniper shots and mortar rounds. Over time, the monotony of daily patrols made their danger seem less real to me.

Of all things, ankle sprains were my biggest concern. On the uneven terrain, I would twist my ankle at the most unexpected and inopportune moments. I'd be sauntering along, and then with one step, my foot would hit a rock at just the wrong angle, my ankle would buckle beneath the weight of all my equipment, I'd hear a faint popping sound of ligaments, and with a surge of nausea, my body would collapse to the ground. It happened to other guys as well, especially on night patrols. The worst places for it were the waist-high alfalfa fields, which masked the deep ridges plowed into the rock-hard clay below. Eventually, this weakness for ankle sprains taught me to be slow and cautious when taking steps anywhere. To this day, I move much more intentionally than I did before going to Iraq.

One day, we were wrapping up a patrol when one of our vehicles hit an IED landmine made of two 155mm artillery rounds wired together. Several of us who were walking in front of the vehicle caught the main shock. It was sudden and loud. My knees buckled beneath me. I felt nausea and an impulse to vomit. I didn't vomit, nor did I urinate or defecate, which are natural enough things to do involuntarily when you get shelled. Mind you, there would have been no shame had my body reacted that way. Stumbling from the blast, I tried to run away. I threw myself to the ground, as taught at Basic Training. I stood back up. A wave of thick smoke drifted over me from the stricken vehicle. There were sprinkles of moisture in the smoke that I at first took to be droplets of someone's blood. The vehicle rolled to a stop with the two men in it hanging out from the hatches. I braced myself with the expectation that they were dead and that their torsos beneath the hatches would be shredded like spaghetti. Happily, however, they were dazed and otherwise intact. (The droplets of blood I thought I felt had actually come from the one guy's Gatorade bottle that disintegrated in the blast.) The vehicle had pivoted away from the IED just as it hit it. Had they driven over it directly, the track would have exploded, taking the rest of us with it. During the following minutes, my thoughts turned to the First City Troop. I thought about the younger guys who joined the Troop after me and wondered if it was worth it, exposing themselves to this kind of danger. The following phrase kept cycling through my head: "This should never happen; this should never happen," which I guess meant, "People shouldn't be trying to blow each other up." I then had the orthodox Christian thought that "wars happen because we live in a fallen world."

Next, we all took cover on the ground, watching the wood line, expecting a follow-up attack and ambush. My thoughts cleared. I now felt stone cold and hyper-rational. Oddly enough, Sherlock Holmes came to mind because I'd been reading a Sherlock Holmes book earlier that week. As I scanned my sector for insurgents, I tried to figure out where the insurgents might be, as if it were a mystery that I could solve like Holmes. A man thinks strange thoughts after experiencing his first anti-tank IED.

It's humbling to experience explosions, to be shot at by snipers, and to be mortared. It robs you of pride because you realize how instantly everything can be taken from you, how a single projectile can kill or cripple you. Since that time, I've received much strength from reflecting on that vulnerability and from absorbing Bible passages like Psalm 91. They've helped with subsequent explosions in life, like when I lost that big client at work, or when that girl in Amsterdam (a six-foot bombshell of another sort) told me she'd finally met the perfect guy, and he wasn't me.

As the weeks wore on, we often accompanied Iraqi soldiers into the field to patrol the area with them. They had little discipline, which made things dangerous for us but at least provided comic relief. There was one American attached to them as an adviser, an old guy from Pennsylvania who had seen action in Vietnam. Back when he first got to Iraq, he looked like beef jerky and seemed so frail that you wondered if he might fall apart any minute. However, within a few weeks in the field, the man bucked up considerably. He gained strength. Though he was 60 years old, he patrolled with those Iraqis as surefooted as an old goat.

On patrol, the Iraqis never walked in formation the way we did. They often had their fingers on their rifle triggers, which made us nervous. Describing their command and control, one of our sergeants said in astonishment, "It's like opening up a box of crickets!" One day, I was standing against a wall with another soldier a few feet to my left. A car was moving slowly down a dirt road nearby, and one of the Iraqis impulsively fired a warning shot across the hood of the car without noticing that we were directly in his line of fire. The bullet struck the wall at chest level, right between my neighbor and me.

Although the danger of our new sector was stressful, nothing wore me down as much as the monotony and sameness of the daily routine. In the Army, we call it the *Groundhog Day* effect, after the movie with Bill Murray. My brain would shift to autopilot, and my senses would blank out for what seemed like hours, the way a computer screen goes blank if you haven't hit the keyboard or shaken the mouse in a while. We spent half of each day doing the same patrol and half the day hunkered down in our armored vehicles. I got so bored with the routine that I started bringing books to read while we sat in the vehicles. As spring gave way to summer, temperatures climbed above 120-degrees. Our uniforms and body armor, which were comfortable at 50-degrees in October back home, became a burden.

Toward the end of our deployment, we got a new lieutenant fresh from Rhode Island. His behavior demonstrated the pitfalls that can easily entrap a young officer. Because he arrived in Iraq just as we were counting down the days left until our departure, he wanted to fit as much war experience as possible into his brief remaining stint. Our sergeants, on the other hand, had been through a lot during the previous year and were understandably eager to take risks only when necessary. At first, the sergeants showed the lieutenant the respect due his rank. "Salute the rank, not the man," they would say. However, after a while, the sergeants started speaking their minds and began to mock him openly. One night when the lieutenant was acting especially cocky, my squad leader took a hand grenade, placed it firmly in the lieutenant's hand, and pulled out the safety pin. The Lieutenant started screaming for the pin, but my Sergeant wouldn't give it to him until the lieutenant recanted all his stupid talk.

Seeing all this made me glad that I was able to cut my teeth as an enlisted man, to witness, from the bottom rung of the ladder, the respect expressed among soldiers seasoned through toil and teamwork and their lack of respect for unseasoned and immature leaders.

Our final assignment, manning observation towers, was in a new sector. We switched from a day shift to a night shift. I performed two tasks, alternating the tasks each night. One was to drive back and forth on a road all night long in a Humvee with our new lieutenant. The stretch of road was two miles long. We drove ten miles an hour, back and forth, in eight-hour stretches. Each time we reached the end of our two-mile road, I performed a three-point turn and then drove back the other way.

At one end of the road, we would always pass a large orange street cone while executing our three-point turn. Those turns made me nervous because insurgents liked placing IEDs inside street cones. The worst was to pass the one street cone that was at eye level. On the other nights, we manned a watchtower by squad. We took shifts, staring out into the night through the NODs (Night Optic Devices), which illuminated the darkness on green digital screens up against the eyes. When the sun came up each morning, the fields and the village around us looked like something out of a Sunday school lesson book, with donkeys braying and shepherds tending them. This final stretch of watchtower duty finally dissolved Erenberg's interest in soldiering—and mine. One night, he took a long draw on his cigar and said, "It's official. As of tonight, I am back in college mode. I no longer give a shit about our mission, and I don't have any interest in the work we are doing." I couldn't have agreed with him more. It was a relief to know that he was as worn out as I was. He said there was nothing to do now but "embrace the suck." That's what they said in the SEAL teams. He said the only antidote to pain and discomfort is to trick yourself into liking it, which is a lot easier when you can share the pain with buddies.

*The watchtower the author's squad manned during their final weeks in Iraq. (Photo by Christopher Pollard)*

Finally, things wrapped up. One day, my sergeant told me to get my stuff together with the other Pennsylvanians so we could go back to Ramadi. Army goodbyes are brief. It didn't take long for me to shake hands with whomever was around at the time of departure. I went back to camp Ramadi and fell in with Pennsylvanians whom I had never seen before during my whole time in Iraq. There was a handful of First City Troopers among them. The Pennsylvanians mostly came from Philadelphia, some from tough areas, but it surprised me how much kinder, less sarcastic, and less abrasive they were in comparison with the Rhode Island guys I had just been with.

# Chapter 35

# Homecoming

As we redeployed home through Kuwait, Mississippi, and finally Pennsylvania, I faced the waves of loneliness and dislocation common to many veterans. How do you carry a vast collection of new experiences that you don't know how to process for yourself, let alone articulate to anyone else? It's one thing to absorb new circumstances as they are come at you, to live in the moment, improvise and muddle through the best you can. It's another thing to analyze and sort through it all once the dust has settled and you have some historical perspective. But the middle place between those two points can be miserable—especially when you have to bear it alone.

Iraq was a big test for whether I "believed" in the First City Troop. Was the Troop an army unit with a bunch of social fripperies added on to it? Or was it a social club with a military appendage? With time, I discovered that the very things that made the Troop seem silly from an army perspective made it a magnificent vehicle for adjusting back to civilian life. Indeed, most military veterans languish because they lack the life-long sense of community the Troop provides.

When our plane touched down at the Philadelphia airport, a small crowd of people gathered to greet their loved ones. After breathing arid Iraqi air for so long, my nostrils caught the heavy humidity of summertime Philadelphia with a new appreciation. Just as they had after basic training, life's simplest pleasures now became thrilling luxuries. Driving a car anywhere I wanted, not having to wear a combat uniform every day, not having to wear heavy body armor, walking around in flip-flops and shorts felt like floating on air. Nevertheless, the tour left me with some quirks and bizarre carryovers from all those patrolling duties.

At first, I couldn't go anywhere without constantly scanning my surroundings, always on the lookout for things that "didn't look right." I found myself instinctively bracing for explosions, sniper bullets, or other unforeseen attacks. When walking down Philadelphia streets, I would scan rooftops, keep an eye out for places to take cover, and pause before stepping around corners with the same sense of alertness that I had weeks before in Iraq. All this didn't feel like paranoia but more like a sense of warrior craftsmanship.

Many soldiers bought motorcycles after deployments, seeking access to adrenaline after having grown accustomed to physical danger. My version of that was to slowly pedal my bicycle through Philadelphia's most dangerous neighborhoods while wearing Nantucket reds and a polo shirt. As a semi-rural child, the city had always seemed scary. But now having learned to ignore the thought of getting shot in Iraq, I felt impervious to whatever might happen in Pennsylvania. At night I would drive my tiny Honda Civic at the highest speeds possible, taking corners as sharply, driving up close to the cement barriers on the Schuylkill Expressway, and veering up to tractor-trailer tires to test my internal sense of calm. At other times, I'd be overly cautious, swerving sharply around debris on the road as if they were IEDs, keeping a distance from vehicles that reminded me of Vehicle Borne IED (VBIED) threats.

It was very bizarre to visit the Racquet Club of Philadelphia (RCOP), a beautifully appointed sports club in center city that gave a military discount much appreciated by Active Roll Troopers. During the course of a normal year, we would use the RCOP steam room and showers after final formation on drill weekends, wandering into the magnificent mahogany paneled men's changing room dressed in grubby combat uniforms. The RCOP held a Wednesday happy hour party each week during the summer, which was an anchor social event that attracted lots of singles.

It was very strange to see my fellow Troopers fresh from Ramadi wearing their summer blazers and bow ties as they stood around all the other people who seemed unchanged from the year before. You could instantly differentiate the Ramadi Troopers because their faces were drawn and gaunt around the cheekbones and eye sockets, in sharp contrast to the slightly puffy office-worker civilian look that everyone else seemed to have. For a while, it was very hard for me to take anyone seriously who had not been to war, especially males my own age. I didn't feel tougher than anyone in a macho sort of way, but I felt a liberating sense of meekness from having been tested, and from seeing how precarious life can be. Ramadi seemed to strip everything away. Serving as an infantryman— the most basic type of soldier, I carried a weapon but never shot it in anger, was ordered around constantly, often bored and often scared. Each night, I went to bed not knowing if I would be alive at that same time the following day, or if I would have both my arms and legs. When I pulled the covers up over my head and drifted to sleep, I would turn to the Holy Spirit in prayer, and wake up the next day open for new pathways in spiritual growth. The cockier a guy seemed to be and the more confident he seemed about his own intelligence, looks, or strength, the more I felt like I could walk right through him.

Iraq also transformed my behavior towards girls from a romantic perspective. I suddenly found myself generous, buoyant, and less shy around them than I had ever been before. You might say that I no longer cared about outcomes. This manifested most strikingly with Daphne Lenox (not her real name), a girl I'd fancied from first sight the year before. Boy, had she been chilly and stand-offish at first. When I told her I was volunteering for Iraq, she sneered, "Ew, gross! Why would anyone want to do that?" When I returned, however, she treated me like a different person. "You've changed," she said. "You're more substantial. You seem more comfortable in your own skin!" We started playing squash together. Petite and rawboned, dressed in whites of abbreviated cut, she was beautiful to watch on the court. And things developed from there.

# Chapter 36

# The German Boomerang

It's hard to know at which point to end this book about the First City Troop, because the gentlemen of Gloucester continue to teach me so much today. A-Troop, 1/104th Cavalry has deployed twice since I went to Iraq—once to the Sinai Peninsula and once to Kuwait. During those times in the desert, a new generation of Troopers has learned to work together, and to better integrate with the rest of the National Guard. The organization still functions as a haphazard crazy quilt of interesting people doing curious things. New members steadily trickle in, old boys die off all too quickly, once-active stalwarts fall away as they burn out from Troop responsibilities, and long-forgotten characters reappear from the woodwork to re-engage with the fold.

Perhaps it is most fitting to end with a nod to the Boyer Scholarship—in this case, its German branches. The reader may recall that when I returned to Pennsylvania from Heidelberg to join the Troop in 2004, I thought I was leaving Germany behind forever. After the life-changing experiences at Fort Knox and Iraq, my memories of Europe began to fade so much that it was hard to recall ever having been there. But then one day, a bizarre thing happened.

In July, 2006, a month after we returned from Ramadi, that year's Foreign Boyer Scholar arrived in Philadelphia just in time for our monthly business dinner. When he walked into the mess hall that evening, something struck me about the way he was dressed. The navy blazer, the bespoke shirt, the necktie... everything was cut on classic English lines that were much too precise to be the clothing of any Briton. Oh no, such a rig could only be German—*north* German. Before I could complete these mental calculations, the new Boyer shot me a look of surprised recognition from across the room. Immediately, I realized that he was not only a German, but a former acquaintance from Heidelberg! His name was Max.

Max came to the Troop armed with two life experiences that prepared him very well for the First City Troop: he had been a solider in the Germany cavalry unit at Luneburg, and he had been active with an old, liberal, male student corps. Also, he had a sharp sense of humor. His flair for banter made him a blazing success among many Americans who had low expectations about how much fun a German could be. Within months, he could sing more Troop songs than any other junior Trooper, he excelled in horsemanship, and he challenged around him to hold to higher standards of gentlemanly behavior.

(Max' popularity sparked a general admiration among Troopers in all things German—an affinity easily acquired by Pennsylvanians with deep colonial roots. After all, Germans had once been America's first non-British immigrant group. William Penn invited them to Philadelphia in the 1680s, and so many took him up on the offer that Ben Franklin would later fume, "Why should Pennsylvania, founded by the English, become a colony of Aliens, who will shortly be so numerous as to Germanize us instead of our Anglifying them...?" This colonial connection can take amazing forms. In 2015, a foreign Boyer Scholar learned that one of his direct ancestors, who commanded German forces under British hire during the

American Revolution, sired two daughters while his wife was living in New York City. They named the girls "Canada" and "Amerika." Canada soon died but Amerika survived, returned with the family to Mecklenburg, and became the Boyer Scholar's great-great-great-great...grandmother!)

Max' success showed how powerfully the Boyer Scholarship program had come to shape the Troop's culture. Over the years, Foreign Boyers often injected a cultivated tone into the unit that helped counteract the drift away from traditional manners that has characterized American society since the 1960s. Attempts at this preservative influence can sometimes take comedic forms. For example, in 2015, after watching a video about the "Trans-Atlantic" accent once taught at American boarding schools, Swiss Boyer Stefan Burgi challenged Troopers to try resurrecting the speech of Katherine Hepburn and Franklin Delano Roosevelt. There were no takers.

The 21$^{st}$ century influx of Germans didn't stop with Max. When he finished in Philadelphia, his buddy Fritz won the Boyer Scholarship the next year. Again, Fritz had served in the German cavalry unit at Luneburg—the very same unit my friend Martin had told me stories about back in Durham, and he was also involved with a student corps similar to the Saxon-Prussians. It was bizarre to see how the Troop reconnected all these loose ends from my not-so-distant past that I was starting to forget about.

Fritz happened to be a direct descendent of Kaiser Wilhelm. This gave him some fascinating perspectives about European history, since ruling a country had once been the family business. As one of the better bred Troopers on the books, Fritz' charm lay in scrupulous humility. He exemplified the Prussian proverb, "Be more than you appear," which means, "don't show off," keep your talents and abilities hidden, so they can be a surprise when discovered unavoidably. There's a similar saying in Britain: "A gentleman never displays his learning." These concepts meshed well with the aversion to self-assertion that runs so deep in Quaker-formed Philadelphia.

One night at the NCO Club, Fritz sighed, "Your traditions in the Troop are not that old by European standards. I mean, 1774 isn't *that* far back. But I'm amazed at the *continuity* you have here in Philadelphia. With all the wars and catastrophes we've had in Germany over the years, it's rare to find institutions like this which such unbroken succession." I often think about rewarding Fritz for this compliment by stealing a road sign for him from King of Prussia, a Philadelphia suburb—but so far, I've staved off the temptation.

Close on the heels of Fritz and Max came Otto, another German Boyer. Although Otto grew up on a large family farm in northern Germany, his real heartbeat was secretly Texan. He longed for big skies, big sport utility vehicles, big belt buckles, and big helpings of desert. To my astonishment, Otto also happened to be a student at Heidelberg the last year I lived there, and he happened to be a member of the Saxon-Prussian fraternity I often visited and almost joined. In fact, he was there the night I left their house and rode my bicycle home singing *So Puenktlich zur Sekunde*.

And so it came to pass, seven years after leaving Heidelberg to join the Troop, the Boyer Scholarship returned Heidelberg to me through the Troop, just like a boomerang. I found myself driving down the familiar old Schuylkill Expressway on a hot, muggy Pennsylvania summer night, with

Otto and one of his visiting fraternity buddies dozing in the back seat of my Subaru. Looking back in the rear-view mirror, I shouted for them to sing *So Puenktlich zur Sekunde*. Without missing a beat, they started singing, belting it out at full volume, just as if they were standing on their chairs back home.

# Further Reading

1. *Albion's Seed: Four British Folkways in America* by David Hackett Fischer (Oxford University Press, 1989). This book describes the four main ethnic groups that founded British North America. Fischer's section on the Delaware Valley is a great starting point for learning about the Philadelphia culture that birthed the First City Troop.

2. *Campaign of the First Troop Philadelphia City Cavalry—April 25–November 11, 1898,* by James Cooper (Hallowell & Co., 1898). Cooper's account of the Troop deployment to Puerto Rico during the Spanish American War.

3. *Democracy in America,* by Alexis de Tocqueville (The Library of America, 2004). One of most perceptive and influential books ever written about American society. Tocqueville borders on prophecy.

4. *First to Fight: An Inside View of the U.S. Marine Corps,* by Victor H. Krulak (Bluejacket Books, 1999). Interesting book from a First City Troop perspective because a Trooper, William Ward Burrows helped establish aspects of Marine culture that continue today.

5. *For These We Strive: The Philadelphia Light Horse and American Identity,* by Thomas Buck Marshall (Williams College Honors Thesis, 2009). Written by the grandson of a First City Trooper, this college thesis provides an illuminating description and analysis of the Philadelphia Light Horse during its founding generation. I wish it were in circulation as a book.

6. *Gentlemanly Power: British Leadership and the Public School Tradition, a Comparative Study in the Making of Rulers,* by Rupert Wilkinson (Oxford University Press, 1964). Although this book is about the leadership ethos once taught at British boarding schools, it has surprising carryover to the First City Troop. Manners and assumptions rooted in the British public school and

American prep school traditions, which have vanished from American society, still survive in muted forms within the Troop.

7. *The Great War and Modern Memory*, by Paul Fussell (Oxford University Press, 1975) Fascinating description of life in the trenches and the horrors of World War One, primarily from a British perspective.

8. *History of the First Troop Philadelphia City Cavalry: From Its Organization November 17, 1774 to its Centennial Anniversary November 17, 1874*, by the 1st Troop of Philadelphia Cavalry (Hallowell & Co., 1874). Official Troop History, volume one—our go-to source for the Troop's historical details.

9. *History of the First Troop Philadelphia City Cavalry: 1874 to 1948*, by the 1st Troop Philadelphia City Cavalry (The Winchell Company, 1948). Official Troop History, volume two.

10. *History of the First Troop Philadelphia City Cavalry: 1948–1991*, by the 1st Troop Philadelphia City Cavalry (The Winchell Company, 1991). Official Troop History, volume three.

11. *The Holy Bible.* Like my ancestors who brought this book with them to the New World, I can't imagine facing anything on earth or in eternity without it.

12. *The House of Morgan: An American Banking Dynasty and the Rise of Modern Finance*, by Ron Chernow (Atlantic Monthly Press, 1990). Superb corporate history of JP Morgan, a great banking house with strong Philadelphia (Drexel) roots, and many Troop connections.

13. *Invisible Philadelphia: Community through Voluntary Organizations*, compiled and edited by Jean Barth Toll and Mildren S. Gillam (Atwater Kent Museum Philadelphia, 1995). Includes handy descriptions of many private organizations in Philadelphia, a number of which were founded by First City Troopers.

14. *Manliness and Morality: Middle Class Masculinity in Britain and America, 1800-1940*, by J. A. Mangan (St. Martin's Press, 1987). Mangan describes Victorian and

Edwardian concepts of masculinity, some of which continue to exist in the Troop today.

15. *My Philadelphia Father,* by Cordelia Drexel Biddle (Doubleday & Company, 1955). Entertaining biography of Anthony J. Drexel Biddle, Sr.

16. *My Utmost for His Highest,* by Oswald Chambers (Barbour Publishing, 2000). A gift from my mother, this classic Christian devotional accompanied me to Basic Training, Iraq and later, Egypt. Chambers served as an army chaplain in World War One.

17. *Past Imperfect,* by Julian Fellowes (St. Martin's Griffin; Reprint edition 2012). A fellow Trooper brought this novel to my attention. Some of the nuances described about England in this book relate to modern Philadelphia, albeit on a much milder level.

18. *The Pennsylvania Associators, 1747–1777,* by Joseph Seymour (Westholme Publishing, 2012). A history of Pennsylvania militia units during the Revolution, with details about the Troop's performance at Trenton and Princeton. The author deployed with the Troop to Bosnia.

19. *The Perennial Philadelphians: The Anatomy of an American Aristocracy*, by Nathaniel Burt (Little, Brown and Company, 1963). This portrait of "Old Philadelphia," written by Burt between the years 1956 and 1962, is still the most exhaustive reference for matters of local culture. Its relevance in the Troop remains strong. At my first Troop dinner, old Joe Harrison (a man in his late 90s) brought this book up in conversation, describing Burt as "the fucking bastard who came to the Armory, acted friendly to everyone and then trash talked us behind our backs!"

20. *The Philadelphian,* by Richard Powell (Charles Scribner's Sons, 1956). A great read, this novel describes Philadelphia sensibilities through a series of life choices the main character makes. A First City Trooper makes an appearance early in the story, as the main character's illegitimate great-grandfather. The book was made into a Hollywood movie, *The Young Philadelphians,* starring Paul Newman.

21. *Philadelphia: A 300 Year History*, by Russell Frank Weigley (W. W. Norton & Company, 1982). A history of Philadelphia, compiled from a series of academic essays. Nicholas Wainwright, a First City Trooper, acted as associate editor and content contributor. Wainwright also wrote a number of books about local institutions, such as the Philadelphia Contributionship.

22. *Philadelphia Gentlemen: The Making of a National Upper Class*, by E. Digby Baltzell (The Free Press, 1958). Survey of Philadlephia's gentry, with fascinating descriptions of certain suburbs and how they developed. The prose is overly academic, but Baltzell described the Troop in good detail.

23. *Storm of Steel*, by Ernst Juenger (Penguin Classics, 2004). Brutal account of combat in World War One, which read to prepare myself mentally for Iraq. Needless to say, Iraq for me was nothing like the Western Front was for Juenger.

24. *The Private City: Philadelphia in Three Periods of its Growth*, by Sam Bass Warner, Jr. (University of Pennsylvania Press, 1968). Describes how Philadelphia was shaped by private organizations during the course of its development. An eye opener for anyone who wants to understand private organizations in the region, and the Delaware Valley's historical preference for small local institutions over centralized government planning.

25. *Puritan Boston and Quaker Philadelphia: Two Protestant Ethics and the Spirit of Class Authority and Leadership*, by E. Digby Baltzell (The Free Press, 1979). I discovered this book as a senior in college, and it explained a lot of things that always puzzled me about our region. Required reading for anyone who has just moved to the Philadelphia area.

26. *Six Frigates*, by Ian W. Toll (W. W. Norton & Company, 2006). This book is about the early U.S. Navy, but it describes the United States and Philadelphia as First City Troopers would have known them during the years leading up to the War of 1812. Quite a few Troopers became officers in the early Navy or joined the Troop after serving in it.

27. *Suburb in the City: Chestnut Hill, Philadelphia, 1850-1990*, by David R. Contosta (Ohio State University Press, 1992). In-depth history of a fascinating neighborhood that contributed many Troop members over the years. The author describes the Troop as having once been the male equivalent of the female debutante tradition.

28. *Washington's Crossing*, by David Hackett Fischer (Oxford University Press, 2006). In-depth account of the battles of Trenton and Princeton, with details about the Troop's reconnaissance work.

29. *With the First City Troop on the Mexican Border: Being the Diary of a Trooper*, by George Brooke (John C. Winston Company, 1917). Brooke's account of the Troop's deployment to the Mexican Border is fun for Troopers to read because so much has changed since then—and so much hasn't.

30. *With the Old Breed: At Peleliu and Okinawa*, by Eugene B. Sledge (Oxford University Press, 1990). A simple and haunting account of the war in the Pacific, written by a World War Two Marine. I read this book during the train-up for Iraq, hoping to steel myself for what was to come. Happily, my experience in Ramadi bore little resemblance Sledge's.

31. *Wooden on Leadership*, by John Wooden and Steve Jamison (McGraw-Hill, 2005). Wooden's bottom-up approach to coaching, stressing the need of attention to small details, is similar to what First City Troopers learn as privates when they go through basic training.

Made in the USA
Middletown, DE
04 October 2016